Enjoy your book whenever and wherever you like!
WITH THIS BOOK YOU HAVE ALSO
PURCHASED THE EBOOK EDITION

1. Go to www.campus.de/ebookinside.

2. To obtain your free ebook, please enter the
   following **download code** into the space below.

   »E-Book inside«:   PYD2X-66DUU-JG2TF

3. Select a **format** (MOBI/Kindle, EPUB or PDF).

4. Fill in the form with your email address and
   click the button at the end. You will then
   receive your **personal download link** via email.

T0364134

DO EPIC STUFF!

RENÉ ESTEBAN

DO EPIC STUFF!

Leadership after Change Management

TRANSLATED FROM THE GERMAN
BY JOHANNA ELLSWORTH

Campus Verlag
Frankfurt/New York

ISBN 978-3-593-51195-5 Print
ISBN 978-3-593-44378-2 PDF
ISBN 978-3-593-44377-5 EPUB

Cover design: total italic, Thierry Wijnberg, Amsterdam/Berlin
Cover illustration: © Shutterstock/Odua Images/Shutterstock/Jatupornpongchai
Typesetting: Publikations Atelier, Dreieich
Fonts: Minion and DIN
Printing: Beltz Grafische Betriebe GmbH, Bad Langensalza
Printed in Germany

www.campus.de

Contents

Chapter 7
Go Big or Stay Home: Now You Will Deliver

Chapter 8
Explain it to a 7-Year-Old:
Simple Communication

Chapter 9
Do it, or Else Nobody Will:
Assuming Responsibility

Do Epic Stuff! is dedicated to my wife, Melanie,
and my two daughters, Emilia and Alicia.
May you always do what makes you happy.

Introduction:
Almost Anything Is Possible with This Book

Do you feel like jumping right in without much ado? Here are three basic assumptions and one promise:

Change management with its methods that haven't changed for more than 25 years has become obsolete. That's the first assumption. Handling changes has long since become a daily process in large corporations and no longer presents any real challenge. If the top of the crop are to come aboard, you must offer them a greater purpose and greater incentives than the prospect of somehow managing the change of the month.

The second assumption is: What's really important for today's corporations is to have teams of highly motivated people focus on big goals and to jointly achieve those sophisticated goals. In this book I call these big goals *epic stuff*. To achieve goals that constitute a leap and not just a small step – that's the true new challenge. Many people will fail simply because there is so much risk of failing: no budget; not enough people; a lack of confidence in oneself and the goal; poor communication; a counter-productive culture; a lack of the willingness to take on responsibility, just to name a few reasons.

The third basic assumption is: Inspired focus is the most essential aspect in order to get epic stuff truly on the road. Whatever we focus on is where our energy flows to. Today, one of the things people find hardest to do is to stay focused and concentrated for any longer period of time. Distractions and diversions are lurking everywhere. The temptation to lose yourself in one thousand and one activities instead of sticking to *one* major objective – I am talking about *one goal* – is huge. Yet inspired, enthused and motivated people still manage to do so again and again. Hence the inspired focus.

And now my promise: If you read this book, which admittedly is not the slimmest book around, you'll have all the tools for epic stuff at your fingertips. Then you can be a leader who accomplishes epic stuff in his or her environment and with his or her people. (Almost) anything is possible with this book. And I mean that just the way I've written it down here. For it doesn't matter at all which branch you're working in, what your market looks like, who your people are or how big your budget is – whether you will achieve your big goal depends little on the goal itself but mostly on how you approach the matter.

In this book I will share my knowledge about how to reach big goals with you, no matter what exactly your goal is. In principle, that's nothing new because change management has also always claimed to be the perfect toolbox for any form of change. What's new is the realization that the factors that are decisive for success are different from those many leaders still focus on. Therefore some details mentioned in this book may surprise you at first. But then you will realize that they are true: The way we think, our belief systems, our focus or the power of our positive vision have a far greater effect on our success in leadership than we used to think.

I didn't invent anything written in this book but rather observed, tested and confirmed it repeatedly at work. That fact lets me begin each chapter with an eye-opening story that is always based on facts. In addition, I talked to leaders who practice *epic stuff*. Don't worry, you won't have to work your way through boring interviews like those you've read a thousand times before and would probably skim through anyway. Instead I had conversations with top executives and entrepreneurs – including s shaolin master – that were inspiring and at times rather personal, complementing and deepening each chapter.

My conversation partners were:

- David Jeans, owner of Beganya Business Services and Partner, FocusFirst, former SVP, Merck Life Science (Chapter 1)
- Kathie Starks, Branch Manager and Head of Asset Servicing, Bank of New York Mellon, and Frank Sielaff, Founder & Managing Director, entrusted former Director Digital Media, Merck Group (Chapter 2)
- Kai Czeschlik, CDO, Allianz, and Yuan Lu, Director of the Shaolin Center of Qi Lu in Schorndorf, Germany (Chapter 3)
- Walter Gunz, Co-Founder of MediaMarkt, and Susann Kunz, Director Brand Strategy and Business Development, adidas (Chapter 4)
- Martin Stork, Head of Workforce Enablement, BASF, and Klaus Straub, former CIO & Senior Vice President Information Management, BMW Group (Chapter 5)
- Dr. Christoph Hüls, Internal Entrepreneur in Action, Merck Group, and Nils Stamm, CDO, Deutsche Telekom & Board Member Münchner Kreis (Chapter 6)
- Daniel Szabo, CEO Körber Digital & Founder YOU MAWO, and Dr. Joachim Jäckle, former CIO & Global Head of Integrated Business Solutions, Henkel (Chapter 7)
- Axel Löber, Senior Vice President Global Brand & Marketing, E.ON, and Jörg Hellwig, CDO, Lanxess (Chapter 8)
- Ludwig Askemper, Managing Director of Mondelez Austria, and Dr. Rahmyn Kress, Henkel X Ventures & Founder Henkel X, as well as Dirk Ramhorst, CIO & CDO, Wacker Chemie (Chapter 9)

I want to take this opportunity to thank all of these fantastic conversation partners. I enjoyed every minute of each and every conversation. I was always able to feel the enthusiasm that motivates these different individuals.

And now I hope reading this book will inspire you and let you focus on your own goals!

Best,
René Esteban

Chapter 1

Head of Epic Stuff: You Want to Make a Difference, Don't You?

"Let's have a talk," Florian said to Alex. They were standing in the break room of the marketing department of a south German DAX Corporation they worked for. It was early afternoon. Florian – the youngest member of the department – had just fixed himself a cup of green tea. Alex, his immediate supervisor, preferred an espresso. "Sure, let's talk," Alex replied with a smile. He was curious to hear what was on Florian's mind. Leaning casually against the counter, Florian looked at him; his gaze was open and friendly. His body language signaled: I'm in the here and now, feeling fine. The young man was the latest super talent of the marketing department! The company had hired him just three months ago. The whole team had been overjoyed that this likeable guy with his lightning-fast perception and fresh ideas would start working with them. They were one hundred per cent sure that the top of the crop among their competitors would also have snapped up Florian without a second thought. Lucky them!

"Well, Alex, I've been doing some thinking," the super talent continued after taking a sip of tea. "And I decided that I don't want to work after all." – A pause. – "I mean, I don't want to work in business. What I'd love to do is advocate for endangered animal species. Or the people in the African refugee zones. It doesn't have to be for money, either. I'll get by somehow. Well, anyway, I'm going to quit this job. Sorry."

Florian's tone of voice was cheerful yet completely sober. Alex didn't notice the least bit of tension. Florian sounded as if he was standing in front of one of these windows of an Italian ice cream parlor, changing his order: "Scusi, Signore! Stop! I don't want strawberry cheesecake. I'd rather have a scoop of cookies."

How did Alex handle the situation? He needed a moment to collect himself. About three seconds. Twenty-one, twenty-two, twenty-three. Then he said to his still-super-talent and soon-ex-worker on the latter's possibly last day of work:

"Whoa, that comes as a surprise, Florian. Let me take a deep breath first! – I hope – and I mean it – that you'll find your *purpose*. If not here with us, then somewhere else. It doesn't really matter where. As long as you don't waste your life doing something that doesn't have any meaning for you. Too bad that we couldn't provide the right framework for your personal meaningful experience here with us. I, just like everybody else here, really enjoyed working with you. But I'd be the last person on Earth to put obstacles in your way if you want to leave. I can't wait to hear what you'll end up doing. But whatever it is: Do epic stuff! And enjoy every single minute of it for life is short. And thank you for enriching our team for three valuable months."

Was Alex disappointed? Certainly a bit. Most likely any leader would be in that kind of situation. Was he angry at the young man? Not in the least. It would have been totally beside the point anyway to reproach him. And absolutely useless to try to talk him out of it or to resist his wish to resign. All that would only have shown that Alex, well, actually anyone in his company, had failed to notice the signs of the times. In fact, they had all realized for quite a while that times have fundamentally changed.

Today you will hardly find any courageous workers who will do what the boss says just because he – or she – is the boss. Employees are motivated by the meaning and purpose of their work. Either your company provides them with the framework that matches their personal meaningful experience, or you can forget about doing any epic stuff with them. Everything else – money, more money, even more money, more authority, corner offices, USM furniture, platinum corporate credit cards – is hardly an incentive any more. All these are only accessories many of them will be happy to take as well. What matters to a growing number of people in the working world, especially those of the young generation, is the *purpose*.

> Employees are motivated by the meaning and purpose of their work.

However, Florian – who is not a fictional character, though his name is different in the real world – does take the easy way out here. Nothing against looking after animals or working to help refugees. But within your remit you, as the supervisor, can naturally convey a meaningful experience much more directly than Alex, the marketing director. And what if you are a manager in a corporation who is facing a global mammoth project without knowing how to motivate workers in 60 affiliates in other countries without having direct authority? These are exactly the starting positions this book is all about. And today purpose is what counts in situations like this one as well! The first thing you get to do is to convey a meaning to every single super-talent you need to achieve epic goals in large corporations. Why is that? What happened in the last few years?

Look, Maslow is standing on his head!

Whenever I think of the world my grandparents lived in, I still picture Maslow's hierarchy of needs in the classic form of a pyramid – a pyramid like those found near Giza: with a wide bottom and a narrow tip. The idea of having food to eat was the foundation. For that you needed work, because only those who had a job earned money and were able to buy food. The next requirement was the need for safety. No more wars! And by God no more inflation, either! Family bliss and spending money on yourself for a change? A nice thought if you had time for that. But self-realization and purpose, the tip of the pyramid? What was that supposed to mean? That didn't make any sense to my grandparents. Today's generation, however, thinks nothing of turning Maslow's hierarchy of needs upside down: What used to be the tip that only few could afford to reach at all is now the very foundation. These days no child in the developed world is able to fathom that anyone might not have enough to eat. Their greatest challenge is the candy shelf by the cash register: a tough test for any child's ability to resist temptation. They get their first smartphone at the age of seven. Our power of imagination doesn't fail when picturing the idea of self-realization but rather that of wars, food shortages and suffering. After all, these days such things only happen in videos on the internet! Our world is a bed of roses, at least for most of us.

In a situation like this one, people turn straight to self-realization. They start to look for meaning. Of course not every coffee break is used to contemplate the meaning of life – no more than sometimes late at night at the bar, after a few drinks. Yet if we take a closer look, we'll find that today just about everybody is looking for something that will give their life meaning and makes them happy and content. Some find their purpose in life at an early age, others not until they are 70 or 80. But there is hardly anyone anymore who doesn't care what happens to him or her in that short period between birth and death. To have at least survived, to hopefully have kept one's family largely intact – these priorities have virtually disappeared in highly developed societies.

Today we want to do more than just survive and pass on our genes to the next generation. Some people find meaning in the study of religion and philosophy. Today anyone can go to Tibet and become a monk at the age of 22. Yet even those who are not really interested in religion and philosophy want to grow and be part of something greater. This has enormous consequences for companies and their employees.

I am deeply convinced that it is one of the deepest and most fulfilling experiences for any human to achieve big goals together. If companies manage to create a framework that inspires people to make most of themselves and realize their dreams, these companies will create epic things with the support of their highly motivated employees. Yes, even those who combine their meaningful experiences with corporate goals will still be working. Yet in that case it will be work without pressure and stress but with ease and joy and inner balance. We may radically reconsider leadership: Every company and every team first and foremost needs a mission. Teams are managed with meaning, with goals, with values, with purpose. I've been fortunate enough to repeatedly witness in recent years how teams in large corporations create great things if the purpose is the right one.

> I am deeply convinced that it is one of the deepest and most fulfilling experiences for any human to achieve big goals together.

On the other hand, I have experienced more than once how everything is deflated if employees no longer see any meaning in their daily activities after the umpteenth change project that was rushed through. "Pressure will only trigger counter-pressure, causing people to give priority to their own security," says Carolin Adler, Transformation & Change Manager of Körber AG, with whom I talked about the future of change management while working on this book. "In that case there is frequently no energy left for the actual change," Carolin analyzes. Yet she says with conviction, "Things are finally changing! With inspiring magnets, such as positive target images, and with designs of the future that are geared towards solutions, we have already got much better results. People want to work and make a difference while having a purpose and fun at work."

Today, even job postings don't really work any more if they only describe one area of responsibility and list the qualifications and work experience expected of applicants. This is where purpose should come in! What are the things a company offers to their future employee so he or she can experience meaningful work, get appreciation, experience the joy of success? Does the job make the applicant part of something great – or merely an insignificant cog in a poorly oiled machine? Our labor market has for a long time worked to the advantage of employees. Not only HR executives know that; everybody does. If you want the top of the cream for your team, then offer them the opportunity to achieve big goals together – otherwise your job posting will only be briefly scanned and clicked away.

Is that what makes the new generation tick? The mysterious Generation Y? The Florians of this world? Yes and no. For a long time the desire of corporate employees to find meaning and reach big goals has no longer been limited to a certain age group. A lot has been written about the "millennials" – yet today the brightest minds of the generation between forty and their mid-to-late fifties think just like their younger colleagues under 35. They are up to date and have adopted the new values. At times this means that new and old values come together in one and the same team. Or they meet in the course of a merger that merges two different cultures. These are exciting challenges!

Starting with a 5-star experience

The employees of a global textile company had never before experienced anything like that: Each one of them was welcomed individually by a driver dressed in a dark suit, carrying a sign with the company logo and their name, at the "arrivals" gate at the airport. They were picked up by a sleek limousine waiting directly by the exit and driven through rolling hills and dense forests to a luxury hotel by a lake in lush nature. From the hotel you could see the lake and a mountain range on the horizon. Every guest was personally welcomed at the reception. Check-in had already been taken care of; everybody could go straight to their rooms. Bellboys carried the suitcases and unlocked the employees' rooms. They were greeted by a large fragrant flower bouquet on a table. A card made of fine paper was propped up against the vase, welcoming them with these words handwritten in ink: "We hope you had a good journey and will enjoy your stay. We are looking forward to having you here for the next three days. Your Workshop Team." There was also a small printed brochure with the exact schedule for the following days as well as information about the hotel, the meals, and sports and fitness activities it provided.

After settling into their rooms, some of the employees wondered whether they were dreaming. They knew these kick-off workshops introducing them to the next change project all too well! Usually they would get the address of some concrete hotel block near the exit of the highway by email and had to figure out themselves how to get there. When they arrived at the hotel, they had to ask their way around until they finally ran into their colleagues. Then they would learn bit by bit from the others what had been planned by "the top" for the next days. Now some of them almost felt like Hollywood stars as soon as they had arrived. Or at least as if they had moved up to the board. What had they done to deserve this kind of luxury, attention and appreciation? And some of them noticed that the term "change" had not yet been mentioned at all. Instead, the invitation to the workshop had read:

> You're in this workshop because you've already achieved great things. We appreciate what you have contributed so far and are proud of you. We will set ourselves a big goal in the next three days. Together we will then reach this goal. For this we'll need your special skills. We're counting on you!

What was that all about? Wasn't the plan to make one team out of two teams in Germany as part of the group-wide digitization strategy "Impact 2030"? And wasn't that a classic change project? Yet no one spoke of "change". Instead everybody talked about a "big goal".

The next morning, just before 9:00 a. m.: One employee after another filed into the room where the workshop was to take place. The large windows provided a magnificent view of the lake and the mountains. The room was decorated with fresh bouquets of exquisite roses that emitted their subtle fragrance. Soft lounge music was playing. Everyone who came in recognized colleagues from their own team – and looked into just as many strange faces. They had to be "the others", the members of the previously separate department, the people they would have to work with and get along with in the future. And they would have to do that in a totally new structure: without e-procurement and e-commerce being separate, as they were used to, but in a new, larger team, working for a unified digital trading platform. No one could really picture it yet. At first everyone sat down among their old team members, so that there were two groups in the room. Calmly watching this development, the management team of the workshop didn't seem to mind for the time being.

Clarissa, a member of the management team, warmly welcomed all participants. After a relaxed warm-up round she asked everyone to sit down with a member of the other team, forming teams of two. Now the partners were encouraged to interview each other: What were your greatest successes in this company so far? Why do you like it here? What do you enjoy most? What's your personal passion? Afterwards everyone presented the results of their interviews to the group. Everyone listened attentively. Many participants had tackled these questions for the first time in a long time. And they learned a lot of new details about people they had been working with for years.

Then Clarissa surprised the group again. She said, "Today each one of us is going to spend all day completing one single slide with four boxes." She pushed the button on the remote control of her MacBooks and projected the four-box slide on the wall. "In the first box you'll write down how strategically important you in your role as an employee are for the whole company." All over the room, people were raising their eyebrows. "Don't worry! You'll help each other, and we'll help you, too, to find that out and to phrase it. The second box is for your greatest challenges. What are the toughest nuts? What are you afraid of? Please be honest! The third box is especially important. This is where you write down your personal purpose. Why are you here? Why go through all this trouble? What do you expect to get out of it? Each one of you has his or her own ideas about the purpose of your work – and we invite you to write them down. And your three greatest priorities will be entered into the fourth box. What do you – and only you – want to contribute to the making of the most successful team for digital purchasing and sales of all times? Your three major contributions to our big common goal. – All right? Then let's start!"

Appreciation will make the impossible possible

Later this textile corporation actually managed to do what many other companies would fail to achieve: In no time the two teams, who had had separate areas of responsibility and different cultures, grew into one dream team that created one of the most profitable digital platforms of the sector. The team members became a close-knit community and reached their big goal. There was a lot of laughter. Stress was rare, and if they did encounter stress, they quickly came up with constructive solutions. Yet the preconditions had been rather bad: The Procurement Department had consisted mainly of senior employees, who had been used to the same processes for many years. There was a flawless command-

and-control culture. By contrast, employees in e-commerce were younger, used to fast innovation cycles and much more intrinsically motivated. Talking about purpose was almost as natural as looking at the quarterly figures.

In order to bring the two teams together and focus on one common big goal, the corporation did things differently than might have been expected. It put – as described – the reward of a 5-star experience at the beginning instead of the end. (Of course there was a reward at the end, too – they celebrated it at Lake Garda in Italy.) All employees were able to feel right from the start: You are valuable, we appreciate your previous work, we count on you. One would think that a perfectly organized travel experience that covers everything was nothing special. In this company – as in many others, too – only the boardroom had, however, previously enjoyed the fact that staff took care of everything while staying in the background.

This time, already the transfer to the hotel created a wow effect. For once it was true luxury and not just the usual business standard. The organizers took care to appeal to all senses: wonderful views, pleasant scents, discreet music, velvety paper. Of course all of that cost a bit of money! But what do a few bills from hotels, printing companies and limousine services matter when that kind of framework creates a dream team that increases revenues and earnings to previously unknown heights? In fact, the new platform of this textile company didn't just double or triple its sales compared to the previous e-commerce department but multiplied it. Other teams around the world later followed this German example.

Here, the people alone were the key to success. It was the appreciation for their individual contribution. And it was the invitation to each one of them to gain clarity about their own personal purpose. An appreciation of the past played an invaluable part in the beginning. Everyone came to the first workshop with the idea in mind to face great challenges. Then they first got the opportunity to visualize the great things they had already achieved – and to experience how everybody else also recognized and appreciated their achievements. Traditional change management often lacks appreciation for past achievements. Everybody is just gazing into the future, at the desired result of a change – while devaluing the past of the people involved. For that reason

> Traditional change management often lacks appreciation for past achievements.

alone, it is no wonder that most change projects fail. Anyone who gets the feeling that his or her previous achievements are suddenly not worth much anymore will be demotivated in no time.

In this case it was different. Here it was demonstrated to those concerned as early as in the first round: You're important! You're not just a small cog in the wheel but indispensable when it comes to achieving the big goal. If you weren't here anymore, there would be a painful gap in our team. For most of those who were present, it was a totally new experience to think about the importance of their role in the company for the overall strategy. Most of them used to believe that only those "at the top" thought about strategy. Of course you couldn't blame them for thinking this. According to Taylorism, it is explicitly undesirable for the individual to see the big picture. But in many corporations this very idea is being turned upside down right now. All of a sudden, corporate strategy is everybody's business! Those who don't know how their role contributes to the overall strategy will find it hard to identify their purpose. And without a purpose it will be tough in the future.

Appreciation ran like a common thread through the process, from arrival to kick-off workshop to the party at Lake Garda, where the achievement of the big goal was celebrated in the end. I find it important to emphasize at this point that appreciation doesn't always have to mean a grand gesture. Certainly an epic goal calls for an epic kick-off. But what matters even more are the little things in everyday life that often cost nothing or hardly anything. You could just take a post-it, write "Good job, well done!" on it and secretly paste it on the computer screen of a colleague who's in a meeting.

By the way, what do you notice about this example? Right: A post-it is something physical. Physical things always express more appreciation than an email, a WhatsApp or any other virtual communication. Even the most beautiful smiley can't compete with that – people simply don't care about digital messages. A handwritten card on fine paper not only appeals to an additional sense channel – the haptic sense – but also shows the recipient: You are worthy of receiving recognition in a special way. I personally always have a supply of nice cards. And I write them with a fountain pen – I just love the fine and elegant handwriting you get when using a proper nib!

> Physical things always express more appreciation than an email, a WhatsApp or any other virtual communication.

I'm probably not telling you anything new when I emphasize that appreciation of employees only really works if it's authentic. So thank them when you're truly grateful. Think about what you really value about an employee's work, what impresses you or what you have learned from him or her. Then share it with them. The more specific and personal your expression of appreciation is, the better. In addition to individual appreciation, I also find it important to always emphasize the common ground. So your message may be: You're great – and as a team, we're even greater!

Everyone in my professional network who has done epic things in the past years works with a purpose, appreciation, and the common ground. As does the South African David Jeans, 54, young in spirit, with whom I met for this book to talk to him about his experiences. David is a former member of the executive board of an international Merck Group company and describes himself as a MUG – the abbreviation stands for "modest unassuming gentleman". As you can see, no one needs to be an extroverted "go-getting" manager who performs wild dances to motivate his team to excel. Other things count. David can tell you just what they are.

The highest level of motivation despite a difficult market situation

I meet David Jeans on a wonderful spring day at the restaurant "Hammermühle" near Darmstadt, Germany. It is already warm enough for us to sit outdoors. We order coffee. The sun is shining on our faces and the birds are singing. We are surrounded by old half-timbered houses that have been carefully restored. I can't resist them, so I get up and take some pictures with my iPhone. Then we start to exchange our views. David smiles his unique bright smile. Sunshine, lovely surroundings, good coffee and the prospect of a stimulating conversation are enough to make him happy. He doesn't need anything else. After sitting down again, I immediately jump into the topic of "epic stuff": that we were all born to create something great. And not to drag ourselves through life for 80 years doing mediocre stuff. And I say that I'm also thinking about David's own career with Merck. In my view David has already done really epic things. How did he do that?

At first David remains the modest gentleman. "Maybe," he says, with extreme understatement, "I should tell you a bit about my principles and values first. How I see things and what I believe in. For me, ultimately, everything depends on value systems. The common mindset of the people you work with, indeed of the people you interact with, is crucial." I nod. I can only agree. Our values and beliefs are always the foundation on which

> Our values and beliefs are always the foundation on which our future success is built.

our future success is built. In particular, the values and beliefs of the people who are around us every day have a decisive influence on whether we achieve great goals or not. "My three most important values are authenticity, integrity, and respect," David explains. "Business is always about people, no more, no less. As long as I stick to these three values, I can really get on with people. That's the most important thing I've learned on the way. We don't live in an ideal world, but if you live the principles that you really believe in, then you automatically attract the right people. Actually, there is no right or wrong. But I want to focus my energy on achieving something with people who share my values."

Anything is possible if "the arrows point in the right direction" – this is the image David is offering me now. He emphasizes how important the beginning is if we want to make a difference with others: Do we understand each other? Do we share essential values? Is the foundation sound? If you want to create epic stuff, you need a positive boost and that synchronous inner alignment right from the start. David is just as convinced of that as I am. "First, try to understand," Stephen Covey once wrote. "I believe in that, too," David affirms. "If you start by understanding where people are coming from, you show them that you respect them. Then give them plenty of time to gradually recognize and accept different views. We're all constantly learning from each other. No one owns the whole truth. That attitude creates the necessary trust. Does that make sense to you?" Absolutely. One of the strongest points David seems to have as a manager is getting people on board and quickly creating a positive, shared spirit. When I want to learn more about it, David first of all remembers his South African origin: "In Africa, we have the word *ubuntu*. Literally translated that means: *I am because we are.* That describes what teams are all about: No individual is more important than the team as a whole, working to-

> Anything is possible if the arrows point in the right direction.

wards a common goal. So I believe in *ubuntu* – because of my African roots as well."

Getting other people involved so as to achieve big goals together – that's what companies are really all about. In good times that sounds easy though even in good times it isn't easy. But what about when the going gets tough? At Merck, David found himself in a situation where his team was suddenly far behind regarding sales. The market had collapsed for a number of reasons Merck didn't control. David got pressure from the top: The group management board expected the turnaround as soon as possible. So what did David do?

"First of all, you should know," he says, "that in our team we're not people who work top-down. So everyone in the team needed a *why*. Why take an extraordinary effort in the next weeks to earn more money again? Our answer was: Because we owe it to our customers! We are there for our customers, for nobody else, and we want to do our best for them again. When the *why* was clear, we started to define milestones, actions, responsibilities. Next, it was important to get everybody involved: operations, IT, internal procurement, and so on. After all, everyone was on board with equal rights! So the goal was clear to everyone, and then there were monthly milestones, feedbacks, team meetings, always with the big goal in mind."

For the moment when the big goal was to be reached, David had devised something spectacular for his team: a joint trip to the Victoria Falls. To a European like me, who has seen a lot of the world, that doesn't sound all that spectacular at first. Yet David explains to me that hardly anyone in his team of South Africans had ever been abroad before. Most of them didn't even have a passport! The Victoria Falls, located in Zimbabwe, about 750 miles or just under two hours by plane from Johannesburg, are among the African wonders of the world. Many South Africans have always dreamed about seeing this gigantic natural spectacle live. "Most members of our team were looking forward to the journey of a lifetime," David says. "The closer we came to our goal, the more momentum was building up. We used the anticipation, the energy, to give full throttle to reach the goal. The Victoria Falls were the carrot, of course. But then we also had the *why* and the intrinsic motivation. You should've seen what was going on after we had reached the big goal! First of all, we helped everyone in the team to get a passport. Then we chartered our own plane! On the day we started on our trip we all wore blue T-shirts we had designed specially for the occasion. Everyone was staring at us at the airport: 100 overjoyed people in blue T-shirts on their way to their own charter plane! When the plane took off, everybody shouted hurray. It hadn't been planned; it was totally spontaneous. I still get goosebumps when I think about it."

The moment David says it, I get goosebumps, too. It was pure joy, David confirms. An epic moment! By the way, for about half of the team members it was the very first flight ever. Such epic moments are possible if the start is successful! Again and again David goes back to the beginning, to the values, the convictions. For him, the courage to do great things comes from your convictions. At the same time, it's important to him to take the initial doubts and fears the team members may have seriously. "In the beginning, I always spend a lot of time listening and discussing things," David says. "You listen to people and understand their perspectives. You feel their fears and doubts. At the same time you show them your own perspective and what you think is possible. You acknowledge the challenges. You accept that at the beginning not everybody may be ready yet. But you show them a common path. There, if you like, is that *ubuntu* again. Of course, nobody would be able to do it by themselves – but together we can even achieve things that seem impossible! The sum of the parts is what makes the difference."

Together, the greatest goals can be achieved – as long as the purpose is clear, the *why*. At the same time it requires people like David, who are authentic and who lead the way with the power of their convictions. Like David, these new leadership types aren't tormented by fears or doubts. Yet they don't think of themselves as being better than everyone else in the team. They know that their perspective is just one of many potential perspectives. And yet they see more quickly than others where the shared journey can lead to. They see what's possible. They have a strong belief that big goals are achievable. Just like David, respect is enormously important to them. They don't want to force anyone into doing anything. But they have the will and ability to listen to people, to get them to come aboard and to align them with a common goal. They lead the way!

It's up to you: You go first!

It's just the two of us. No one in your business knows what you're thinking while reading this book. Right now there is only you and this book with its ideas and concepts, stories, examples, and interviews. Now that we're alone, I'm asking you directly: Do you want to do something big in your company? Do you want to be the "head of epic stuff"? Would you like to experience similar epic moments to those David and many others you'll get to know in this book have experienced? Or do you prefer to be just average? Do you like to go with the flow, adapt to and do what your bosses ask you to do? Probably not, right? I mean, who wants to be one of the whiners who later complain that their careers were so exhausting, that their jobs were never fun and that nobody ever appreciated them?

If you continue to read this, I assume you have long decided to do epic stuff. Maybe you're already doing epic things and now just want to do it in an even greater style? That's even better. Are you curious how others have done it and what you can still learn? That's exactly what this book is there for. Either way, I'm glad you're part of the crowd.

Okay, we've just clarified that. So now I'll tell you the most important principle needed to make things epic in large companies. It is: *You go first!* Everything depends on you. *You* will have to take the first step, because if you don't, little or nothing will happen. David Jeans has got to the heart of it: A team will only achieve great goals together. But for that commonality to come into being at all, for everyone to have the same mindset and align themselves like arrows on the target, it needs – *you*. Creating the energy necessary for the start is the first and most important task of any leader. And to put it quite bluntly: You don't only show the other members of your team where to go. You yourself always go first. You're the signpost that moves along. Signposts usually don't do that – but you do. Brian Tracy once said, "If it's to be, it's up to me." That hits the bull's eye. When I dream of something, there is no one but me to make my dream come true. Epic stuff starts in your head. You will read more about that in the next chapter.

> *You* will have to take the first step, because if you don't, little or nothing will happen.

What exactly *is* leadership that "goes first"? What's important? First of all, as David Jeans has said, it's important that you have clarity about your own values and beliefs. You may ask yourself: Am I honest and authentic? Am I unafraid but rather full of self-confidence? Do I want my team to do much more than the team members feel up to? Do I see a possible way that will lead to the big goal that others can't see yet? Or that they think is less realistic, too risky or too much of a challenge? After all, you know that if you stand up in a corporation and say, "We could do something big," you'll meet resistance at first. The naysayers will be in top form. The enviers, too, if you're unlucky. You won't stand a chance if you do things only halfheartedly. However, if you're one hundred per cent sure that the opportunity is there for the taking and the road there can be overcome, then resistance won't be an issue. You'll stay firm, saying, "I'll do it now, and if we do it together, it'll work out, too. Every one of you can contribute something. Let's talk about our common ideas. I want to listen to all of you." That will quickly do away with resistance. Now everyone can admit whether they want to contribute to the common goal or not.

If people put as much energy into the start of something big as they put into badmouthing ideas, voicing concerns or complaining about other people, they would surprise themselves. Recently, I went to a DIY store to buy a grinder and some special oil for a worktop, but I didn't really know what to look for. Within thirty minutes I ran across three totally different employees. The person at the information booth said, "You'll have to ask the people in the other departments." And where are these departments, please? A finger pointed

> If people put as much energy into the start of something big as they put into badmouthing ideas, voicing concerns or complaining about other people, they would surprise themselves.

vaguely in the north-northeastern direction. The salesman in the power tool section turned out to be a real pro. He asked me detailed questions about what I was planning to do and recommended the right tool. Pleasant, professional, and committed. Then I went to the oil section. I had to ring a bell to alert the sales personnel. Ten minutes later a salesman appeared; his expression seemed to say, "So who's bothering me now?" It was so obvious that he didn't feel like working that it was painful for me to ask him anything at all. The product he finally recommended turned out to be the wrong one.

Corporations are just like this DIY store: There are many annoyed employees who either don't want to work or don't know anything – or both. It's best to just leave them alone and not try to change them. You can't do epic stuff with them. Find the one out of three who is totally motivated, loves his job and knows his purpose! How that works? It's easy: If you're courageous and authentic, if you stand up and clearly communicate what your big goal is, you're going to attract the very people who share your values and feel like going on a long journey with you. This is the principle of resonance, whose subconscious mode of action has been psychologically tested: You start to laugh, and at some point everyone will be laughing. A flash mob is dancing in a public square, and more and more people will start to dance.

For the principle to work, you must be visible. You have to show everybody else that you are excited and motivated and ready to go ahead. Is it going to be a walk in the park? No. But why should it? What is exhausting and painful once in a while will give you more energy in the long run. Mountaineering is more strenuous than a walk around the small lake down in the valley – and incomparably more satisfying. You can feel the endorphins. You are expanding your limits. Your self-esteem grows. As you keep expanding your limits, the radius will increase and you can do greater and greater things. Together with your team. Everybody keeps going a small step further. And again and again: You go first!

> As you keep expanding your limits, the radius will increase and you can do greater and greater things.

If you're going to do it anyway, you might as well make it big

"Head of epic stuff" – that was what Clarissa became in her textile company in the end. Worldwide! Together with an external consulting firm and two colleagues, she, who had a PhD in economics, initially merged the existing e-procurement and e-commerce departments at the company's headquarters in Germany to create a pilot for a new, digital platform for products and raw materials. She had started with a 5-star experience for all members of both teams that had still been separate at the time. Already after the kick-off workshop everyone in the future team knew their personal purpose. They knew that each and every one of them would play a pioneering role that was hugely important to the company's future strategy. That knowledge alone released a powerful boost of energy. The older employees, who were used to command-and-control, quickly began to adapt to their younger colleagues. Soon everyone knew what they had to do and what their greatest priorities were.

When the beta version of the new platform was already running smoothly at the company's headquarters, it came to a gigantic merger. The group took over an approximately equally strong Italian textile company. Now, Group Management Board member Clarissa had an even bigger job to do: She got to establish new teams for integrated digital purchasing and sales for all divisions of the expanded group, this time not only with members of the previously separate teams of her company but also with the people from the previously independent Italian company. A huge challenge! For two years Clarissa lived and worked all over the world – in Europe, in Southeast Asia, in North and South America, in South Africa. Her recipe for success was the same everywhere: to get everyone involved, to listen to everybody, to define the purpose. To show that each and every one of us counts. To get their commitment to big goals. And again and again: to lead the way. After two years, the new platform with its decentralized teams around the world generated nearly half a billion euros in sales.

> Today corporations rely on people like you. People who believe in themselves and their purpose and who are willing to set themselves big goals over and over again.

While doing so, Clarissa found that "epic stuff" knows no cultural differences. Nor gender, religious or ideological, or any other significant differences. Everywhere in the world, people want to experience purpose and grow. And you can find people who would rather make a big contribution than a small one everywhere. Of course one size smaller is always okay, too. But only those who have done something great are really proud of themselves afterwards. "Big" is always relative, that's for sure. So by defining "big", we are defining "epic": Big goals are goals that demand a lot more from us than we are used to. They definitely take us out of our comfort zone. Typically, in the beginning, almost everyone but the person going ahead as the leader is skeptical of whether the goal can be achieved at all. In any case, it is perceived by all as being extremely challenging. There is also an actual risk of failure. It takes courage. In the end, however, everyone is not only rewarded with a great sense of joy but also with great inner growth. Epic stuff is the stuff that will be talked about in the company for years to come.

Today corporations rely on people like you. People who believe in themselves and their purpose and who are willing to set themselves big goals over and over again. We live in a time of rapid innovation that is strongly based on start-ups. For large companies, it is no longer enough to do a little change management every now and then. Companies may as well delete the term "change management" from their vocabulary. Not just because permanent, complex, and rapid change has long become mundane and this change is no longer "manageable". But also because now it's really important to achieve big goals. And to do so with the current employees. Some large companies think they can solve all their problems by acquiring start-ups and incorporating them. Most realize after a while that this doesn't work. Instead, it is important to raise the creative potential of their own employees and to rekindle their workers' passion for goals. I believe companies who can do that can do anything!

In the end, it's always about freedom. The more self-control we have and the higher the degree of freedom is, the greater is the happiness factor. The most powerful companies of the future will succeed in setting a framework in which people can grow willingly and fearlessly on the basis of purpose. These people will enjoy creating something great, so as to serve the company, its customers, stakeholders, and society. And because it makes them happy, too. Nobody needs to explain to them why they should start working early in the morning or why their work needs a certain amount of quality. All they need is a framework in which to unfold, as well as highly motivated leaders who lead them with courage. Epic stuff is created where there is a purpose and freedom and cooperation. But what is the first step along the way? It's the confidence that you can create something

> The most powerful companies of the future will succeed in setting a framework in which people can grow willingly and fearlessly on the basis of purpose.

great in your business. Most people are enormously limited by negative thoughts and outdated convictions. If you believe in yourself, if you have a clear vision and are absolutely sure that your vision can become reality, then you will leave everything behind that has limited you in the past. That's what the next chapter is about.

Chapter 2

Think (Yourself) Ahead:
Success Starts in Your Head

"Introducing unified software throughout the corporation takes five years and costs a minimum of 50 million," Roger said. His expression was like that of an employee of the municipal public order office when writing tickets. The atmosphere in the conference room plummeted immediately to the freezing point. Anne's face that always showed a soft and friendly smile even in the most heated discussions froze. Wolf, who had just taken a cookie out of the bowl sitting in the centre of the conference table and had taken a bite, stopped chewing. The chewing process distorted his features in a peculiar way. Carey leaned back in her chair and relaxed. She looked directly at Roger and asked, "Says who?" Roger grinned sarcastically. Instead of looking at Carey, he let his gaze wander over his colleagues sitting in a circle. "Well, who do you think? Number One a. k. a. 'The Matador'," Roger said coolly. By that he meant her CEO Javier, a native of Spain. His confrontational nature had earned him the nickname "Matador" – which he himself didn't know, of course.

Although the atmosphere in the room was tense, Carey stayed totally relaxed. She looked at Roger frankly and kindly. Then she said, "If Javier really thinks so – what I'd like to hear him say himself – then we'll just convince him that it's not true. With solid preparation, we can do a roll-out like that in six months. And in terms of budget, we are sure to stay within the single-digit millions. We're going to prepare a plan now and we'll present it to

Javier in two weeks." Roger objected immediately, "That's a waste of time! We'll never get the budget for that; Javier doesn't want it anyway – and besides, it won't work." Chewing again, Wolf interjected, "Hold on! Carey, didn't you manage to do a roll-out like that in your former job with our favorite competitor?" Carey nodded. "Right. It even took us just four month." The idea seemed to thrill Anne. "I think Carey should tell us more about it," she said. "After all, she's the one in the room who has the most experience with something like that …"

Does this situation sound familiar to you? It probably does, right? In my experience, it reflects a typical day in the culture of many organizations. Someone thinks big, makes a bold suggestion – and someone else immediately fires off their killer phrases: "That's impossible, you can't do that, it will fail for sure, it takes too long, we don't have the budget for that, you won't get away with that, the board has long since decided against it, blah blah blah …" Frequently they then call upon a higher authority in support of their own criticism. Of course the bosses and all the experts feel the same way as the skeptics do. Have you ever wondered if there might be a pattern behind such recurring situations? And if yes, what pattern? Actually there *is* a distinct and very powerful psychological pattern: Whenever there are generalizations, belief systems are involved. The pattern consists of the fact that someone's particular belief is not to be questioned. For that reason they use a generalization and claim that it's valid without even examining a specific situation and the actual chances and risks involved more closely.

You probably know at least one person like Roger – as usual, the name has been changed – who will, whenever a courageous step would be the right one to take, show the same knee-jerk reaction: "That won't work anyway!" How can they really know that without trying it? The answer is simple: They can't know it. All they want is that a certain belief, which they usually were talked into believing very early in life – most likely during their childhood – should remain valid. Such belief systems can, for example, be "Be careful!" – maybe their mother always said that? Or "A cobbler should stick to his last" – perhaps one of their dad's favorite phrases? Their family might also have had the conviction that "pride goes before a fall". So don't you ever tempt fate!

When such subconscious beliefs cause someone to drive with the handbrake on, to have little self-confidence and to never fully realize their potential, this is termed "limiting belief systems". Carey seems to be completely free from such restrictions. She leans back, relaxed, and says, "We'll do it, and we'll do it in half a year!" Carey believes in the feasibility of the goal and in her own abilities. She has already mentally programmed herself for success. If Roger was the manager in charge, the project would probably take five years and cost 50 million – as long as he wants to believe that. He may also realize his limiting beliefs and decide to change them.

Success always begins in your head. And with the very decision what you want to believe. It depends on the imagination, the determination and the optimism of the responsible manager whether a big goal is a castle in the air – or already a mental reality. This goes far beyond classic change management and represents a real change in the mind*set*. Today, it's no longer enough to cope with a change that is triggered more or less externally. It is rather about taking on the full responsibility for big goals and understanding that it's primarily up to you to decide whether this goal will be achieved or not. In practice, these major goals will sometimes be identical to what used to be called "change project". Naturally some people will keep using that term for a while. What matters, however, is one's inner attitude. And what it is begins with the question of whether limiting belief systems are involved.

> **Success always begins in your head.**

The handbrake in your head has a release button

As soon as we're in this world and have let out our first scream, we are surrounded by belief systems. Our parents, our family, our entire social environment – everyone believes in certain things, thinks something is possible, something else is impossible, considers this kind of behaviour desirable and that kind undesirable. Children subconsciously adopt these beliefs. As adults they might never reflect on what they absorbed in their childhood. Whether their subconscious beliefs will benefit or hinder them later on in life is purely coincidental. It depends on what beliefs are involved and what goals the adult pursues in his or her life. Maybe someone grew up in an entrepreneurial family that was convinced that "courage will pay off". As an adult, that person starts his or her own company, takes risks and succeeds. Someone else may grow up in a family that believes that "life isn't fair". The adult person tries to make it on their own, too – and promptly fails.

Sometimes I think: It's crazy how much power parents have over their children! We put all sorts of things into our children's heads, things that later manifest themselves in their lives. For good or bad – unless the children later discover their own power and decide to consciously control their own beliefs. I myself adopted a lot of limiting beliefs in my parents' home, too. For example, while I was still going to school, my mother would say to me, "Your brother is the athlete in the family, but sports are not your thing; you're more artistically talented." And wham! There it was, right in my head: "I'm no good at sports." And I had another problem as well: At school I didn't only have mediocre grades in sports but in arts and music, too! Based on my mom's conviction, I was supposed to be really talented in these subjects. So if I wasn't even good at what I was supposed to be good at, then what the heck *was* I good at?! It was already working, that handbrake in my head.

As an adult, I was able to get rid of these beliefs. Yet that sports issue was darn stubborn! For many years I never felt as physically fit as I would have liked to yet at the same time I thought that doing sports wouldn't make sense anyway. The conviction "I'm not good at sports" left over from my childhood had me firmly in its grip though I didn't even know it. It was only when I dealt with beliefs during my coaching training that I realized what was wrong with me. I deleted my old belief and started exercising immediately. In no time I reached the goals of my training plan – because I was now focusing on training without thinking about the generalization whether I'm athletic or not. Today I'm much more relaxed about sports. I don't think I really need a six pack. But that's my own decision. I've experienced myself how powerful limiting beliefs can be and how easy it is to overcome them. All we have to do is decide to believe in something else. That's all. It always helps to see how others have already managed to release that handbrake in their heads.

Since male athletes ran the first 100-metre sprint in the 19th century, the 10-second record was considered to be unbreakable for over a hundred years. But on October 14, 1968, the American Jim Hines ran the 100 metres in 9.95 seconds at the Olympic Games in Mexico City. The spell seemed to have been broken. However, it took almost another nine years before that record of under 10 seconds was topped: On August 11, 1977, the Cuban athlete Silvio Leonard covered that distance in 9.98 seconds. The altitude of Mexico City is 7,546 ft; Leonard ran in Guadalajara, which is still almost 5,250 ft high. The thin air reduced the aerodynamic drag, making it easier for the runners to make that last tenth. At sea level Carl Lewis was the first sprinter to break the 10-second mark on May 14, 1983. In 1989 three athletes were faster than 10 seconds. In 1997 that number had increased to five. In 2003 that mark was undercut six times, in 2008 ten times. Today it is still rare but no longer a sensation for an athlete to run one hundred metres in less than 10 seconds. Sports scientists attribute this not solely to more effective training methods or better nutrition. The elimination of the "mental threshold" is just as significant. In other words: Athletes today no longer believe that it's impossible or nearly impossible to run 100 metres in less than 10 seconds.

So what does that mean? Take care of your limiting beliefs before you even think of doing epic stuff in your business! First get rid of your own. Then take care of those of your team members. It's not that you couldn't do anything with the people in your company who are inhibited by limiting beliefs. On the contrary, you will find many hardworking and loyal employees among them. But if you want to achieve the big goals, if you want to push boundaries and go farther than most people have the self-confidence to do, then you will need people whose minds are liberated. People who say, "Well, okay, pretty challenging. But we can do it anyway." Again, the principle you already know from Chapter One applies: *You go first!*

You may start with your own beliefs. Ask yourself: Who am I? What motivates me? What did other people in my life make me believe in regards to overcoming hurdles and achieving big goals? What do I dare to venture? What do I think is possible? How much do I trust others? How do I deal with setbacks? Try to remember what shaped you. Did anyone in the past – your parents, teachers, superiors – say things to you that you still believe today? Is there something that you fear, something that shouldn't happen under any circumstances? Questions like these will guide you to your beliefs. It's best to get a coach. An experienced coach will help you to discover, verbalize, and eventually dissolve your subconscious beliefs. The dissolution means that you decide to believe something else. You can also reinforce your new decision with affirmations and anchor it in your subconscious mind. Lets suppose you heard your parents say over and over again, "Be careful or else something will go wrong!" In that case you may want to repeat the following affirmation for a while – in front of the mirror in the morning, while jogging or when you're sitting in your car by yourself: "I'm courageous and always safe." Or "I'm as successful as I decide to be." Working with affirmations is like doing a house-cleaning in your head. You eliminate your limiting beliefs and replace them with powerful new thoughts. Today almost all elite athletes work with affirmations. It's part of the standard reper-tory of mental coaching for pros.

It's a bit more challenging to recognize your team members' limiting beliefs and to help them change their convictions. Of course you won't position yourself in front of the whole team at a kick-off meeting and ask, "Who believes we can't do it? Raise your hands!" You must first gain your team members' trust before talking about beliefs. After all, you want to get to their deep-ly rooted and largely subcon-scious patterns of behaviour. This only works when people open up. And that in turn happens only on the basis of trust. You can also hardly speak about beliefs in a group but only in one-on-one talks. David Jeans, with whom I spoke for the first chap-ter, said that he always takes a lot of time at the beginning of big projects to have long talks with everyone in the team. This time is spent well.

> Today almost all elite athletes work with affirmations.

Once you have established a trusting relationship with some-one, you can cautiously approach his or her beliefs. Not directly but rather indirectly: That's the trick! You create an emotional setting by talking about visions, for instance. You ask them what culture it takes to realize the shared vision. You ask what people want and what they dream of – for the team, for the organization, and for themselves personally. And then you ask questions such as, "What could stop us?" Or "What's the worst thing that could happen?" If the trust is there, if you're really empathetic, and if your approach is slow, then you will get close to their limiting be-lief systems. Then people will open up and talk about what they're secretly afraid of or what they don't have the self-confidence to do. Then you can work together. Show your counterpart your perspective. Reveal what makes you so relaxed and optimistic. Your most important employees may then also want coaching so they can work on themselves. Enable them to do so. It's an indispensable basis for epic stuff to reflect on your identity, values, beliefs and typical reaction patterns. Katherine Starks, called Kathie, manager at Bank of New York Mellon, with whom I met in Frankfurt, is aware of that, too.

Everything a person really believes in can happen

Kathie Starks and I are sitting in "Gallo Nero", a superb Italian restaurant near the Old Opera House. The restaurant is not all that big and very tastefully decorated. Gold-framed mirrors and beautiful paintings adorn the walls painted in a soft red. The tablecloths match the walls; the tables are set with candles. We are served by attentive waiters. Kathie just had a delicious turbot, and I had pretty much the best sea bream *ever*. We continue to sip the sparkling white wine we ordered to accompany the fish, and I'm delighted that she's ready to answer a few questions for this book. Kathie is Branch Manager and Head of Asset Servicing at BNY Mellon, a global bank. I've known her for a while now, and I've noticed that she approaches big goals in her own special way. You might call it "carefree" in a positive sense. Kathie looks relaxed and confident, even when her goals are super demanding. I'm interested in how she does that. Is it a special personality trait that lets her always believe in her success?

"Well, I was raised a bit differently than most people," Kathie explains. "Even though my childhood was in the 1960s." For the most part, these were still authoritarian times that only slowly moved towards openness and self-realization. So what exactly was it that her parents did differently? "Specially my dad always told me that I could do anything I wanted. Even when others said that this was something only boys could do. Our parents even bought toy cars for us girls. And we were allowed to wear jeans, just like the boys. We didn't have to wear dresses like all the other girls had to in those days." So Kathie's parents let her do her own thing, and when she wanted something, it was all right? "Yes, we were raised a bit 'anti-cyclically'. Yet my father always expected us all to become doctors or lawyers. Well, that didn't happen. But what my parents taught me was that anything can happen if I want it and really believe that it'll happen."

When it comes to being successful and achieving big goals, you can hardly ask for a better belief system. I ask Kathie how it affects her in business today. "Well, I started in the new company, and from Day One I was convinced that we'd be successful," she says. "I knew that the previous four years hadn't been very successful and that many employees were frustrated. But I didn't pay any attention to that. I think it's like a virus. Believing in success is contagious. Soon some of my colleagues started to think and talk like me. After a few weeks everybody did. From then on everyone believed that we'd be successful." Was it just Kathie's way of talking to people, or was something else involved? "Actually I think my words contributed the smallest part. I entered a room and knew things would run smoothly. We'd be successful. Apparently I radiated what, to me, was a given thing. That's why nobody doubted it. By the way, I didn't have a Plan B, because I knew that everything would work out anyway. You could say I had this extreme serenity, almost a kind of *fuck-you* attitude, but in a positive sense. Namely that I won't put myself under pressure under any circumstances. I knew things would work out. That's also why I didn't have to work day and night to make things work."

That makes perfect sense to me. Kathie just does her thing even when there are critics – but then there always are. When it comes to criticism, she's resilient. For me, this has a lot to do with mental strength. A personality trait that was not necessarily considered one of the most important success factors in classic change management. I'm curious about how Kathie sticks to her guns. And how she deals with resistance. Kathie considers that question for a moment; then she says, "When I join a new company with my attitude – and by now that's been five or six times – it's always just about the same. I say, 'We'll do this, it will work and it'll be fine.' I will have convinced a few people within a short time. These are the ones I work with. We then define the first strategic issues together. We think about what activities we need for our strategic goals. And then it works like a vacuum cleaner: We suck up the rest of the people. First there are two, then three, four, five, six, and in the end I have a highly motivated team. Sometimes I hear people say about the first team members that they weren't good performers, I should replace them. But I don't care about that kind of talk. My life is about seeing how people evolve. My training in coaching and team coaching helps me do just that."

Impressive. I want to know if Kathie never has any doubts in herself. "Yes, I have", she blurts out. "I'm suffering from 'Impostor Syndrome'." Kathie laughs. "In every new job I wonder why they hired me." Seriously? I'm perplexed. Even if self-deprecation is involved here: Where do her self-doubts come from and how does she deal with them? "It's just at the very beginning, and maybe it's also a typical female trait," Kathie says. "When women apply for a job, they want to be able to do 80 per cent of what's required in their new position. I can only do 30, maybe 40 per cent when I apply for a job anywhere. That's why at first I consider myself a miscast. But when I start working in my job and realize that people are benevolent and supportive, I quickly forget about that. Deep down inside I don't have any self-doubts. And I never listen to the critics but always to the advocates. They're everywhere. You mustn't think: He or she is definitely against me; everybody wants my job. Giving up that kind of competitive thinking is very helpful."

And what if there are real difficulties? "A Swiss friend of mine, who also works for a bank, in a very high position, once told me never to call anything 'difficult'," Kathie says. "Because that sounds as if I can't do it. It's better to call it a challenge. Because I can definitely tackle that. Of course there are moments when I'm not sure whether it will work out with a certain team, a certain company or their products. Then I deal with it with a sense of humor to lift my spirits again. Once I stood in the pouring rain at the railway station and spotted a rainbow that had formed over our office building. I took a picture of it, tagged it with the hashtag #signsfromthegods and used it in a presentation." What a wonderful anecdote! It sounds like emotions are important to Kathie. And that she enjoys to playfully seek confirmation that she is on the right track, rather than dealing with her doubts. "That doesn't mean we never had any conflicts," Kathie intervenes again. "There was a lot of friction in the team – and we welcome that! Creativity and innovation are only possible if conflicts are seen as something positive." That makes sense. What else is important to Kathie?

"The language," she reveals. "I use a very positive language. I also try to speak only positively about other people. For instance, we have a rule in our team: If we have visitors from other countries, specially seniors from our bank, we will always find something positive about any team member that we will say to all those present. Of course it has to be authentic, or else you can forget it. This creates a powerful we-feeling. Another example: There are certain words that I use in my team over and over again. I make it a point to call ourselves 'Team Germany'. For several years Germany used to be a problem for the corporation. Well, that's over now. Now we are 'Team Germany' with great self-confidence. We're the successful team. Words do work."

Away with negative thoughts and words!

What Katherine Starks is saying is another basic requirement for Epic Stuff. When success begins in the mind, it means banishing all thoughts of failure. And that's not all by far. It also means avoiding negative moods and even bad news. After all, positive wording that anticipates the desired future is part of it all. Kathie Starks doesn't say to her team members, "Maybe we'll get a new customer soon. Let's see. The negotiations are ongoing." Instead she says, "We'll have a new customer next month, so be prepared."

Linguistically, she leaves no doubt that the positive, not the negative, is what will happen. This approach may seem radical to you. Isn't it a bit over the top? If you're skeptical, it

> When success begins in the mind, it means banishing all thoughts of failure.

may be because you've never tried to lead yourself and your team on the road to success with positive thoughts, moods, and words before. Anyone who has ever really tried it may still not know *why* it works so well. But he knows that it *does* works. And it does!

The reason for that is this: We don't have to look for negative things in our everyday lives. We are constantly bombarded with negativity. All you have to do is turn on the news on the radio or television or visit any news website online, and you'll get an average of more than 90 per cent negative news. "No news is good news" is the infamous principle of news journalism. Incidentally, this is the reason why I turn down the sound on the radio in my car whenever the news comes on, why I haven't watched the evening news for a long time, and also ignore the homepages of news websites. We are constantly presented with a one-sided image of reality that has a negative filter. None of the many people in your town or region who were kind to each other yesterday, who had fun, who helped each other, who did something good for their kids, who simply enjoyed life, are written about in today's paper. But you'll read about that one purse snatcher, those three burglaries and two traffic accidents that happened yesterday. Positive thinking and talking doesn't mean you're exaggerating. On the contrary: It sets the standards. Most things that happen to most people are positive – yet they still think and talk negatively most of the time. It is not positive thinking but rather the omnipresence of negative thinking that's crazy!

Thoughts and words are so important because in the end they become our reality. You can find these famous sentences already in the Talmud, the ancient Jewish book of wisdom:

> Watch your thoughts, for they become words.
> Watch your words, for they become actions.
> Watch your actions, for they become habits.
> Watch your habits, for they become your character.
> Watch your character, for it becomes your destiny.

Positive and goal-oriented thinking, speaking and acting are essential for organizations in order to achieve big goals. Imagine a project leader who gets bad news – say, on a major construction site, the developer went bankrupt and everything suddenly comes to a halt. The project manager gets annoyed, slams his fist on the table and yells at his co-workers how on Earth this could happen. He curses under his breath and wonders why, of all things, everything always goes wrong in *his* projects. The whole team is petrified and everybody feels down. The next days nothing is moving.

Now imagine another project leader in the same situation. He gets the same message: the developer is broke, the project has been stopped. But he doesn't get angry. He doesn't look for explanations, either, and doesn't take refuge in generalizations why something like that – seemingly – always happens in his projects.

Instead, he simply takes note of the fact. He gathers his team and discusses what can be done. How soon will we get a new property developer? What are the legal aspects? What are the first steps we can implement immediately?

There will be setbacks on the way to big goals – undoubtedly. But the really important question is: How do we deal with it as a team? What's our focus on? It's important to focus on the goal as much as possible, instead of on resistance. Which thoughts and which topics cost energy and which ones give energy? If everyone is always in a bad mood after talking to the controller, you might, for instance, bring in an external consultant, too, who keeps an eye on the financing and periodically conducts this kind of discussion. This way everyone can focus on the goal again without constantly being forced to listen to allegations that everything is much too expensive. People who believe that they are reaching their goals and are busy with how to get there will succeed. As Kathie Starks said, she first gathers those who share this positive belief around herself in each new team. No matter whether they're considered to be top performers and key figures or not. Over time, more and more people will join them. This is valuable advice. The firm belief in the chance to achieve something great fascinates and attracts people. When you stand up and say, "I know it'll work and it's going to be fine," radiating confidence and serenity because you truly believe what you're saying, then you'll attract the people you need, too.

> There will be setbacks on the way to big goals – undoubtedly. But the really important question is: How do we deal with it as a team? What's our focus on?

Nothing is more powerful than your confidence in yourself

Some time ago I stayed at a fabulous hotel in the Swiss Alps. It had a bar with a breathtaking panoramic view of the snow-capped mountain tops. After work I ordered a glass of fine wine at this bar and had a chat with the barkeeper. We chatted about all kinds of things and his job, too. I'll never forget how he said to me, "I have the best job in the world. Just look at that view!" Several days later I was still thinking about what he had said. I wondered: How many of the people in the corporate world with a top-notch education, excellent job experience, and a large paycheck could say "I have the best job in the world"? Of course I know people who think and talk positively about their jobs. But I also meet many, many others who have doubt about themselves and their organization. In Germany, in my view, it's often a problem when people in a company are 100% convinced of themselves and their abilities. When they say, "What I'm doing here is just my thing, and I enjoy every day, every hour and every minute of it," this will quickly create envy in their environment. Or distrust. That bartender in Switzerland showed me that anyone can do what makes him happy. And if he or she has found it, why hide it from others?

If you want to do epic stuff, you should believe in yourself as well as in the goal. Otherwise it won't work. Confidence in oneself can also be felt externally and transferred to others. That's really important. However, one point is crucial: Never believe that you are already everything, know everything and can do everything. This is the arrogant attitude of yesterday's generation of managers, which fortunately is increasingly less common today. Such huge egos and their affected behaviour

> Never believe that you are already everything, know everything and can do everything.

merely annoy the young generation. We all can constantly learn from others and constantly evolve. Imagine there periodically being new versions and upgrades of yourself, as there are of software. You exist as version 1.0, 2.0., 3.0, and so on. Perhaps you only feel like version 2.0 of yourself and would like to be version 3.0. Then it's best to develop 2.1, 2.2, and so on. It's time to grow step by step. The greater the perceived gap to the next version of yourself, the greater your dissatisfaction. So focus on growth in small steps. It sounds trivial, but epic stuff succeeds in small steps. You set one foot in front of the other with discipline until you have reached your goal.

When you stop wanting to be perfect and appear perfect, you will develop true self-confidence and a true belief in yourself. Be like Kathie Starks: When you feel up to 30 to 40 per cent of a task, it's time to accept it and learn the rest. People who do epic things don't think they're the greatest, nor do they consider themselves to be perfect. Instead the programme they have in mind is: I can learn everything if I really want to.

> It sounds trivial, but epic stuff succeeds in small steps. You set one foot in front of the other with discipline until you have reached your goal.

And I can keep growing. It's this combination of self-assurance and willingness to learn that makes people in organizations a magnet for allies and comrades-in-arms. That combination will make you extremely relaxed and create calmness everywhere. No one likes to join people who have a bloated ego and think they know it all and can do everything. Because everyone senses the insecurity that's actually behind it. But if you stand up and say, "I don't know yet *how* we'll do it, but I know we *can* do it. Everything will be fine. We will succeed," then you will attract people who have been waiting for someone to lead with that kind of positive belief.

Provided you really believe it, that is! Just talking like that but thinking differently, secretly being doubtful, won't work. People will sense it immediately. This is the power of interpersonal communication through subconscious signals. It all starts with what you think and feel. Your language will literally correspond to that. Everything you say will be authentic. After all, your actions always correspond to how you think, feel, and talk. "Thinking, talking and doing in harmony is happiness," Gandhi said. People who experience that kind of harmony are relaxed, serene and confident. As leaders, they radiate authority in their team in a very natural way. These people apply that authority to empower their team and develop the individual team members. Only leaders who are constantly developing themselves can initiate the development of others. Nobody likes to listen to people who have stopped evolving. However, those who keep working on themselves and pushing their own boundaries again and again can have a tremendously positive influence on others.

Anyone who is an executive should ensure that everyone in the team also believes in themselves and is convinced they're doing the right thing. Employees also don't need to be perfect but may develop themselves step by step. Therefore the leader starts with himself or herself and then communicates to more and more employees his or her conviction that the big goal can be achieved and that this very team will be able to overcome all hurdles and reach that goal. In the beginning there may be only two or three team members who don't have any doubts about themselves and the goal. Then that number will grow continually. Their serenity and optimism are contagious.

The acid tests for confidence in oneself and the big goal will certainly come. Major goals in organizations can hardly ever be reached without any resistance. If fears and doubts just won't disappear and everyone almost despairs when the first major hurdle appears, then the first question has to be: Is this goal really the right one? Perhaps it's too far outside the comfort zone? Then it's time to readjust the goal. However, once everyone believes that the goal is achievable, the motto should be: Stay tuned! What is now required is resilience. Not to be disenchanted by anything. And to never ever lose sight of the goal. Sometimes you need great perseverance to reach a big goal. For leaders who believe in themselves, giving up is not an option.

One such leader is Frank Sielaff, born in 1975, formerly Head of Digital Media in Group Communications at Merck and current CEO of entrusted, a digital strategy consulting firm. Frank is a prime example of someone who has made epic stuff in a corporation that the group is still talking about after all these years. He initially created a globally standardized platform for internal digital communication. Then he started to work on the company website and adapted it to the newly redefined brand core with a relaunch. Huge tasks that required incredibly many hurdles to overcome. What mental programme let him manage to stay tuned and achieve these great goals?

There's no other idea than to keep going

The Lufthansa conference centre in Seeheim is located on the edge of a dense forest, surrounded by greenery. Here I meet Frank Sielaff for our talk. We're sitting next to a tall glass front and enjoy a great view of the beautiful mountain range called "Bergstrasse". "Success starts in your head" is the topic of this chapter. I want to know from Frank with what mental attitude he has managed, over a period of several years, to virtually revolutionize the entire web architecture of a global and widely distributed corporation. I'm also interested in the attitude the others had at the beginning. Who said right away, "That will work!"? And who said something like, "Forget it, you can't do that anyway"? Such huge IT projects usually mean tall hurdles. To sustain motivation and spread determination and optimism is doubtlessly an enormous challenge to the mental strength of any leader. I ask Frank to tell me a bit about his experiences.

"As far as internal communication is concerned, the corporation was initially quite a mess," Frank begins. "There weren't only countless intranets in the Merck subsidiaries around the world but also very different ideas about how to communicate with each another. In contrast to the relaunch of the website at a later time, regarding internal communication it was also a lot less clear at the start how much we would be able to achieve with our project at all. The conditions were much more challenging. At the time there was no common concept yet concerning what the internal communication at Merck should be about. This concept has developed only through our project."

How was Frank able to start under these conditions? After all, you have to start somewhere. "In small steps," Frank explains. "And the first step was the technology. In 2008, it was first all about how to structure the technical mess. It was not until much later that I started to better understand the organizational and communicative chaos, which went hand in hand with the lack of a uniform technical basis. Since we were so focused on the technology, after the first pitch in front of the IT board we only got the okay for a small solution. We had heated discussions about licenses, budgets, and so on. Nobody campaigned for the big solution. So the small step I got the okay for meant to add to instead of rebuilding the structure."

I want to know more about that: So Frank jumps in with a vision of how things could look in the end and comes out with a maximum of 10 per cent of what he really wanted. Wasn't that a huge setback and didn't he already think of giving up then? "The disappointment came a bit later," Frank says. "At first I was still hoping that the new little tool we were allowed to use would help us to attract and engage more people. But that wasn't the case. First there was a short buzz of enthusiasm and then a valley of tears. People were disappointed. " So what happened then? "In a second attempt in 2011, I had already integrated a communicative concept and set up the whole issue. The fact that we again had a discussion about the budget and everything was reduced to the license costs was another setback. The motivation of the entire team plummeted again. We had already placed announcements in the staff magazine, and now everything was questioned. During that time I collected my strength mainly by telling myself: Okay, that's now a decision of the whole company, and however it'll turn out has nothing to do with how well my arguments were. We then benefited from the fact that the company was about to be newly positioned and our project fit in well with that. In 2013 we finally got the go-ahead for the big solution from the board. But even then it still took two more years to find a supplier who would do exactly what we wanted."

> First there was a short buzz of enthusiasm and then a valley of tears. People were disappointed.

In the end it turned out to be many years with several setbacks. After the go, Frank and his team had the big goal in mind, but they still didn't have the opportunity to start implementing it immediately. How can you stick to something that long that you have your mindset on? "We gradually built up a community for the project within the company," Frank explains. "The exciting thing was to keep the momentum there. About 500 people were involved, and we had to keep them motivated the whole time. It helped us to get support from senior management on a regular basis. In the final phase in 2015, we were then able to really speed up the process." Failure was not an option? "Back then I would generally ask myself: What does failure actually mean? For me, failure didn't mean to deviate from an original plan. Only giving up is failure. Not to stick to my goal anymore. The goal I had in mind was a unified communication platform. That goal was absolutely unalterable. I also asked myself: What would 'not to go on' look like? Okay, you may not feel like doing it anymore. But it's going on go on somehow anyway. I think I've always been good at motivating myself. Of course I would have liked to have everything done faster. But then I got used to the fact that it didn't go fast and told myself: Well, if it won't be done that fast, then it'll be done step by step."

That sounds like great serenity and mental strength for me. Qualities that all executives need if they want to achieve epic goals in organizations. Was there anything else that helped Frank to remain mentally strong for such a long time? "What really helped me was to have a very large network inside and outside the company," Frank says. "I always asked for lots of feedback from others. That concerned both my ideas and the internal perception of these ideas within the company. I knew people I had a real bond of trust with and who also were very good at abstract visions; they could show me where we were at the moment and why we weren't getting ahead. Talks like these reassure me enormously."

Anything else? "Exchanging ideas with managers from similar companies in forums helped me a lot, too. And discussions with peers at conventions were enormously important as well. I could always share something relevant, and in return I learned how the others were doing things. That was very helpful. A great confirmation was when we received one award after another in the U.S., Germany, and even Australia for the project. Then even Microsoft became aware of us, and we started to talk about strategic partnerships. In the end we excelled as the ones who took a giant leap and who are now way ahead of everybody else. You can lose such a lead quickly again; then others will follow suit. But what was interesting was that gap between your own perception and the evaluation from outside. After all those years in which things had been really tough sometimes, outsiders now considered us to be the ones who had just ventured the big solution." Epic stuff? "I guess that's what it looked like."

Having the mental vision of arriving at your goal all along

John Strelecky's book *The Big Five for Life* contains a metaphor that has inspired me ever since I first read that great book. It's the metaphor of a museum. It can be applied both to an individual and a team. At the individual level, the metaphor works like this: Imagine, all your friends, relatives, partners, customers, just everyone you know and have met before, decide to build a museum for you. It's the personal museum of your life. All of the pictures and video installations in the rooms show only you. They don't idealize you, though, not the way you would like to see yourself. But rather the way you actually live. Every day, from morning to night. If you pay attention to people, hug them, do wonderful things with them, then the visitors of your museum will see pictures and videos of these scenarios. If you yell at people, fight with them, get upset, visitors will see that as well. If you spend 80 per cent of your life on things you don't really want, then 80 per cent of your museum will show just that. The museum will open on your 80th birthday, and anyone will be able to visit it and see how you lived.

The purpose of this visualization is to realize what you really want out of life. The idea that everything you do today will be displayed in your museum sharpens the focus on what you actually want to achieve. You ask yourself: Is what I'm doing right now paying into my major goals in life? Or is it a waste of time? Or is it even counterproductive, actually throwing me back? The results of everything you do will hang on the walls of your museum. You can already see them. This metaphor of a personal museum may also be transferred to what you're doing

> You ask yourself: Is what I'm doing right now paying into my major goals in life? Or is it a waste of time?

with your team in your organization every day. How much does that pay into your common big goal? Will, in the end, half of the pictures in your museum be mediocre, depicting anxious, doubtful and discontented people, nagging, criticizing, looking for mistakes and spreading a foul mood? Or will the visitors go from one room to the next, pleased and amazed because only really exquisite paintings are presented? Pictures of people who believe in themselves and their goals and who support and motivate each other every day?

In order to achieve great goals, it's not enough to get rid of negative beliefs and develop a positive vision just once. On the road to your goal, it is necessary to always remember the vision, the goal, the idea of what you want to achieve in the end. There are various methods and techniques how to do that; I will list some of them below. It is not really the methods, however, that matter all that much. Two other things really matter: Firstly, to embed the goal so firmly in everyone's head that a sense of having already achieved the goal can be retrieved. Secondly, to activate this emotion again and again, preferably every day, and to ensure that everyone involved fully aligns their actions with this goal. In a workshop, for example, you can work with your team to find out how exactly it will feel when you reach that big goal. Remove yourselves from the level of pure facts. Focus on the sensory perceptions and emotions you will have when you reach the goal. What will it look like? What will you feel? What kind of music will you listen to?

A good trick, for example, is to decide way ahead of time where and how you will celebrate your success in the end. And do it down to the details. So instead of just saying, for example, that you will celebrate it in Barcelona, you may want to picture that celebration in detail. For example, you decide to celebrate at Hotel "W", which is located right on the beach. You picture yourselves on the rooftop terrace of the hotel tower in the evening sun. The glittering metropolis on one side, the sea on the other. What will you have to eat and drink? What music will be playing? Develop a vision of how it's going to be and focus on it again and again. You may also use a specific tune, a specific song to anchor the final image. What kind of music do most of the team members prefer? What motivates you all? Play that song repeatedly as a signature

> A good trick, for example, is to decide way ahead of time where and how you will celebrate your success in the end.

tune – for example, before or after important meetings. Make sure the lyrics have a positive message, even if they are not in your native language and therefore not everyone in the team can understand every single word. Words are powerful! The song doesn't necessarily have to be "We Are the Champions" by Queen – but it could be.

Another tip: Make the fact that you work on something great together visible in your daily work. Many successful teams have put up posters with motivational sentences or affirmations in their offices. Paint something that illustrates the achieved goal. The motto is "If you think it, ink it". I know a team that built a large, colourful sculpture together which expressed their spirit and kept motivating the team on their way to the big goal. As I said before, what you do with your team isn't really what matters in the end. It is crucial to picture the goal on an emotional basis again and again and then work towards it in a relaxed manner. All the techniques and tricks I have mentioned sharpen the focus on the big goal. And that's just what the next chapter is about: Focus. How do you focus? How do you focus on one goal instead of dozens at a time? And how do you turn off distractions? Epic stuff is always the result of focus. It won't work without focus.

Chapter 3

If You Hunt Two Hares, You Won't Catch Either: Focus First!

When Christopher came into the crowded room, there was an atmosphere that reminded him of a derby between two warring football teams. After the merger of two approximately equally sized companies, this was the first joint meeting between the two marketing departments. There were two camps, sitting separately and throwing hostile glances at each other. On both sides, there were spokesmen who loudly displayed their displeasure, gesticulating wildly. As the director of the Transformation Office, Christopher had been assigned the responsibility for the merger of the two former competitors' marketing departments. The merger had been contested until the end. That was the reason for the highly emotional atmosphere in the room. The union feared the worst and was already spreading horror scenarios via the media. In general, the media response was negative. The day before, the headline in a leading business magazine had read: *This Wedding of Giants Can't Lead to a Good Marriage.* No one around Christopher envied him his job. "My heartfelt condolences for your new job," a colleague had written to him early in the morning via WhatsApp, adding a winking face emoji, which did nothing to lessen the sarcasm of the message.

Yet Christopher appeared totally relaxed. He calmly strolled to the front of the room and leaned against the edge of a table instead of sitting on the chair behind it. He knew the rules for Day One and accepted them: For the time being, meetings could only be conducted under regulated conditions. There were lawyers in the room who would measure every word that was spoken. The employees' emotions were just about as sensitive. It was a frustrating process. Though most of the workers might be willing to work together, for all of them, they and their families came first. If it was inevitable that employees would be fired, then it should be someone else who would be let go. That was everyone's attitude. It was only understandable from the human point of view. Still, Christopher focused on something else. He saw a completely new brand that wouldn't have anything to do with the two previous brand essences. He wanted to bring this new brand to life with the people in the room and carry it out into the world. He derived everything else from this one big goal.

When Christopher opened the meeting, all eyes were fixed on him. He spoke casually, as if he didn't feel the tension in the room at all. After a few introductory words he said, "I didn't come here with any ready-made concepts. We'll find the right way to reaching our goal together. But there is one thing I know for sure: We can do it. Together we'll create a really cool new brand. The only thing I'm asking of you right now is to focus fully on that goal. Let's join forces and resist the temptation to distract ourselves with all the issues that are calling our attention right now but that are obscuring the goal." Towards the end of his brief address, Christopher presented a YouTube video he had prepared. It showed a Rube Goldberg machine. You are probably familiar with such devices, though maybe not under that name. A Rube Goldberg machine, also called a "the-way-is-the-goal machine", is a nonsense gadget that accomplishes a trivial job in many unnecessary and complicated steps. The term "Rube Goldberg machine" goes back to the cartoonist Rube(n) Goldberg, whose cartoon character Professor Lucifer Gorgonzola Butts invented superfluous and complicated machines – for instance, a fully automatic mouthwipe gadget for dinner tables.

In an episode of "Sesame Street", Kermit presents his radio-switch-on machine. Instead of flipping the switch of his portable radio on himself, he intends to let his invention, which he calls the What-happens-next machine, do that task. The machine drops a small sandbag on a seesaw that opens the lid of a box, from which a balloon filled with gas rises, which in turn is attached to the "on" switch of the radio by a cord and finally flips the switch via the lifting force. (In the sketch, however, this doesn't really work and ends up quite surreal with the radio dangling from the balloon, flying away.) Kermit's gadget is a very simple version of a Rube Goldberg machine. There are also highly sophisticated, monstrous devices that require dozens of unnecessary individual steps and therefore a long time to reach a trivial goal – for example, to beat an egg. Of course the greater the constructive effort and the more trivial the result, the funnier such a device is.

You may not only smile about a Rube Goldberg machine but also think about it. Namely when you start to wonder if the operations in large organizations might not be similar to this kind of nonsense device. By showing the video of a nonsense device at the meeting on Day One, Christopher – as usual, the name has been changed – first demonstrated serenity. By doing so, he managed to defuse a heated situation. Most of the people in the room were actually able to smile about it. They received a tongue-in cheek-answer to their burning question: What will happen next? At the same time, the video was also a clear warning of what's going wrong in most large business organizations and shouldn't happen here: There is a lack of focus on the most important, simple and clear goal.

> There is a lack of focus on the most important, simple and clear goal.

Instead, people worry about a thousand complicated issues that grab their attention and unnecessarily extend the road to the goal. If I want to turn a switch in a company, I shouldn't have to construct a new device to do so, the way Kermit did. Instead I'll go directly to the switch and flip it. Makes sense, right?

Keep the most important goal firmly in sight while staying relaxed

Of all the success strategies that an organization can use, focus is the most important one. That's why I say: *Focus first!* When everyone wants too much at once, it will take an unnecessarily long time to reach even the most trivial goals. Or you might even temporarily lose sight of the goal altogether. Anyone who wants to do epic stuff in a company can decide on one single, major goal and stick to it consistently. That's the one-goal strategy. Focusing on an important goal means clarity, concentration and perseverance. It requires stamina from everyone concerned. Initially this will be in serious contradiction with today's *zeitgeist*. Most major business organizations have embraced a culture of too-much. Everyone wonders, "How can I do even more in even less time?" And that's exactly the wrong question. The right question would be: "Which of the things I'm dealing with today will pay into my big goal?" Focus is not about increasing efficiency. It's not about more goals, either. Instead it's about the quality of a goal. Understanding and anchoring this first is critical to epic stuff.

> Of all the success strategies that an organization can use, focus is the most important one. That's why I say: *Focus first!*

When I and my focus consultants first come to a new company, I frequently hear managers say things like this: "My team can't focus properly." By that these executives usually mean that their employees don't carry out their tasks efficiently enough. When taking a closer look, I notice that this isn't the actual problem. In reality, the lack of focus is caused by the fact that the team members are working on an incredible number of topics at once. Frequently it is no longer obvious which topics are more important than others. Sometimes employees are working on 20 issues simultaneously while reducing the quality of all issues to 10 per cent. Otherwise they couldn't manage their workload. When the people involved are made to realize what they're doing, I often hear excuses at first – for instance, that there are all the other business units they allegedly owe this to, or: "I can't help it; I have to do it this way, otherwise I'll get in trouble with X, Y, and Z."

However, the real problem is never "the others". Instead, the problem is always your own indecision. Focus is an issue of mindset. If you don't know what you really want, what you enjoy, and what you want to achieve with others in your organization, then you probably have a problem saying "no" when others are using you for their own goals. And so all sorts of issues will pile up on your desk in no time. Instead of sticking to the one task that's the major issue *for you*! No matter what the others may say. After the merger of two large companies, Christopher was aware of the unique opportunity to create a new global brand. He made that his Number One project and his focus. While everybody around him was still in a flurry of excitement, he was already developing his vision and focusing on his big goal. He knew exactly where he wanted to go. He didn't care that there were colleagues who felt pity for him.

"Our plans miscarry because they have no aim," the Roman poet and philosopher Seneca wrote in his famous letters to the younger nobleman Lucilius, whose mentor he was. And he continued: "He who does not know which port he should run into, will not get favorable winds." That has long been one of my favorite quotes. I really like the image of a ship Seneca uses here, and I like to embellish it a bit for our times. Just imagine that everybody wants to take a sea voyage because they just feel like traveling by boat. That's to say, they apply for jobs in the corporate world because they find it cool to work for a large corporation. At some point they will be on board and will be thrilled when the ship sets sail. Wow! Everything is so huge here on this ship! So exciting and fascinating! They passed the same small island twice already, so they are definitely going in a circle. Nobody has realized it yet. Instead, some start to argue that you could paint the ship in different colours. And you might refurbish the dining room soon. These are all pleasant topics. But which port should the ship sail for? Nobody asks this question.

Sounds absurd? Yes, it does! And yet I know quite a few teams in organizations that seem to be on such an absurd cruise. Everyone is fully committed to their little section of the ship. One manages the weather forecast; another one takes care of the engine room. Every day the passionate ship's cook serves delicious meals, and the ship's doctor is always ready to help. Where the ship is going? Somebody up there on the bridge will know that! – What if not? What if the bridge is empty and the automatic course control is set so that the ship goes in a circle all the time? Because everybody forgot that the course is the most important thing of all? In that case someone should quickly go to the bridge and enter the course. *Focus first!* Determining and holding the course does not mean that there won't be any storms and unpleasant waves. Maybe the journey will take longer than originally planned. You may not even reach the desired port – because it's frozen over – and might have to switch to a nearby harbor. But at least you will have arrived in the right area and be able to cover the last stretch overland. The main thing is that someone set the course and held it. This sounds so trivial in theory yet all too often is not observed in practice.

In many organizations, *one goal*, that one big goal, is a culturally difficult issue, also because hectic activity is considered a quality feature.

In many organizations, *one goal*, that one big goal, is a culturally difficult issue, also because hectic activity is considered a quality feature. Someone will come very early in the morning and leave very late, immediately respond to any mail, skip no meeting, pipe up everywhere, constantly come up with new ideas and make suggestions how to improve traditional operations –

wow, what a dedicated worker! No one has the courage to ask what measurable results all of these frantic activities have in the end. And whether there aren't any more serene and relaxed workers in the company who achieve much larger goals in the long run.

If you want to do epic stuff, you may want to get away from the hectic hustle and bustle and instead learn how to achieve major goals in a focused and relaxed way. This requires a good deal of courage. Anyone in a large company who slows down to concentrate on a worthwhile goal will quickly make enemies of the hectic people around him or her. After all, usually they are intelligent people who are very much aware of the fact that they are merely scratching the surface of the issues. They will always do only things that promise recognition in the short term. And they often know as well how little the company will ultimately benefit from their hyperactivity. If you step out of line and really want to try something new, initially that will be a bad thing for these people and their self-positioning in the corporation. But you can be sure that most of these people would rather have a real purpose than just be busy all the time. Once your ship is on course, you have the chance to change their minds and win them over. But that requires patience.

Over the last 30 years our ability to be patient has greatly diminished. Today we live in an instant culture and want to have everything immediately. Deliveries on the same day are already standard in many areas. We prefer to use the instant messenger to have our message immediately pop up on the addressee's display (unless he or she has temporarily disabled it, as I keep doing) instead of waiting until they have read our email. Yet emails are already faster than their predecessors, letters or faxes that the secretary used to put in a folder and hand over to the addressee. Very few people realize that they are being tricked by the reward system in their brains. Do something at once, trigger something with one mouse click, and already endorphins are released – great! It's like taking drugs. And just as bad. As a leader, you should consider how to make enough endorphins flow on the way to major, long-term goals. This book has already provided you with suggestions how to do that. More tips will follow later in this chapter.

Always start with yourself. Make *focus first* your mindset. Concentrate on your big goal like an athlete is set on winning. Stay tuned and be patient. But please don't tense up! Focus on your goal without spoiling the good mood of others with your doggedness. I call that *soft focus*: staying on that major topic while being relaxed and calm. Christopher demonstrated just that: He knew what his goal was and that he would achieve it with his team. This certainty made him feel totally relaxed. For all his coolness he wasn't arrogant but empathetic. He was calm but not negligent. In the end

> Staying on that major topic while being relaxed and calm.

he reached his goal. It took a little longer than planned. But he did it, and the stakeholders were thrilled. Just like Clarissa, who created a unified trading platform for her sector. Getting a single country involved took her up to eight months. And that at a time when everyone wants to see quick results! She stuck with it and she stayed calm. She kept making people feel that they were doing the right thing, and she rewarded every small step along the way. Clarissa never gave in to the temptation to dodge small issues. And she always kept her sense of humor and her good spirits. That's *soft focus*.

Achieving focused goals that were once considered unattainable

Kai Czeschlik does not act the way I expect a top manager working for an insurance company to act. The CDO who works for Allianz welcomes me dressed in a tie-less white shirt with rolled-up sleeves. We are in a building that looks more like a start-up incubator than part of a global corporation's HQ. "I'm not at all an insurance person, to be honest, and relatively new to the industry," says the 47-year-old father, laughing. Apparently he can read my mind. When Kai joined the Allianz Insurance Group to tackle the big goal of "digitizing the corporation", as he calls it, working on the new Allianz campus was out of the question for him. The building in Unterföhring, which was opened in 2015, has 624,308 square ft of office space in a cool, sophisticated business design. Kai prefers to experience "a certain otherness and, above all, the independence I need", if not even "self-sufficiency", in a different corner of Munich. For him, this has to do with the start into digitization, projecting it to the outside. In Kai's building the dress code is: no suits, no ties – yet proper and compatible with the Allianz style.

Before we talk about how Kai focuses and achieves big goals as a CDO, I'm still a bit curious about his previous career. Kai used to work for Telefónica, TUI, and Amazon before joining Allianz. "At TUI, I had the opportunity to build up the digital business and actually lead a very, very similar company into digitization," Kai says. "That was really exciting. I did that for almost three years. Then Amazon called and asked if I wanted to switch to the European management board to handle everything, I mean *everything*, that has to do with customers." I'm impressed. After all, customer orientation is Amazon's trademark. "Exactly, and with this flagship I was allowed to push things forward. Then I joined Allianz." So much for Kai's background. After all, our topic is focus and achieving big goals. How did he experience that in the different companies? "Well, if I compared Allianz with Amazon, that would be terribly unfair because Allianz is 130 years old and Amazon was born when digitalization started. But if I compare the two anyway, then the first thing that strikes me is that at Amazon, the whole company is more or less pursuing one single goal."

What does everything centre around at Amazon? "Of course, the top objectives are customer satisfaction and loyalty; that's what Amazon stands for, and that's what it carries in its DNA. Irrespective of that, however, it is certainly the value of the shares, the fair value of the corporation. Every employee benefits equally from that, and it prevents competing goals. If I look at the compensation, for example, there is the fixed salary, of course, and there are shares. However, there is no variable compensation based on personal goals. One person's goals could contradict another person's goals. So at one point there would be goals that would cancel each other and that wouldn't be compatible with the one big goal. All of Amazon's employees, however, have the share price as their common goal." So that's ultimately the *one goal* of the entire organization – simple, clear and understandable.

What about Allianz? "As I said, it's not fair to compare the two," Kai emphasizes again. "Allianz is very vertical: a pronounced hierarchy that is lived every day, a high degree of division of labor, many board members. I don't judge that; that's just how it is. In that kind of environment you have different corporate goals per se: One person has a sales target; another one has an efficiency target; the third person has a quality target that doesn't always match the efficiency target because high quality can sometimes be inefficient. Well, and now I'm aiming to make everything digital from one end to the other. For that to work at all, stakeholder management is paramount. I actually spend a good deal of my time here trying to convince everyone else. First we acknowledge how successful a company that makes 11 billion euros in profits every year already is. But then we just tell our story. And that is that we have to reinvent ourselves. We live in an age in which all developments come so fast that nothing is comparable to what we saw in the past 15 or 20 years. The opportunity this provides is to adapt more than ever before to our customers' needs. So you keep expressing your appreciation for what went well in the past. Then you arouse the people's interest in new things, meet them halfway and take them along on the journey. Then you turn your big issue into small digestible bites, and suddenly everything works out. So, stakeholder or people management, that's what it's all about here very often."

Okay, doing everything digitally and focusing on the customer is the big goal. How does Kai focus? And how does he get around to the sub-goals, the single steps he calls "small digestible bites"? It happens often that CEOs or owners of large companies bring in CDOs like him, telling them, "Make us digital, will you?" They don't know what that means and how to go about it, but they don't care, either. CDOs, in my experience, are often left to their own devices and need tremendous self-discipline to focus on what to do first. Nodding, Kai explains, "What corporates aren't good at is setting prior-

> What corporates aren't good at is setting priorities.

ities. They do try to focus on top priorities. Unfortunately they have an incredible number of top priorities, so they'll quickly lose focus again. So, setting priorities and focusing actually is what we do first."

So what exactly did that mean in this case? "Well, the first thing I say is, the focus is on the customer and how he will perceive us in the future and interact with us. We all are very much used to focusing on the customer, as I also experienced when I worked for Amazon. Basically, Allianz already knows exactly where it wants to go; that's the positive aspect. But our products of the past will no longer be those of the future. Presumably we will provide more insurance for situations and certain phases in life. So it won't just be this any more: I've bought my first car and need insurance for it. When I'm facing this kind of total turnaround, my first step will be to look for the most relevant 10 to 15 topics we should at least mentally work on for the next two or three years, yet not as a roadmap but rather agile. First of all we, the whole top management, need to get a sense of what the world of tomorrow will look like."

Kai already said that he focuses on one major issue and then divides it into small manageable steps. He adds how important it is to start small, agile and in sprints, and then to achieve successes and present as well as explain them to the outside world in order to gradually reduce any skepticism. Kai tells me that he is something like the "foreign secretary" but he also has a "home secretary" who backs him up. I just love that image! Particularly the infamous "layer of clay" that contains people who simply want to sit out changes often presents a challenge. In his function as the "foreign secretary", Kai counts on storytelling, tirelessly making efforts to persuade others. But what I can't wait to find out is: Has Allianz ever managed to reach a big goal with a team, even though most employees may initially have been skeptical if the goal really can be achieved? Kai immediately recalls one such situation. I ask him to share it with me.

"Well, insurance is challenging per se; it's an extremely complex business," Kai starts. "Today, you assemble new products from a hodgepodge of components that are part of a product, and you drag them along every time, even when you don't need them for a particular product. This creates immense legacy, making a development process complex and lengthy. We said we want to change that and be able to create, test and establish brand new insurance products within six weeks. We teamed up 40 absolute specialists and instructed them to atomize all components and create a kind of Lego construction kit. First they would say, 'Forget it, that can't be done; we've already tried that a thousand times. Everything is linked together; we can't break it into bits.' We pretended not to understand, asking: 'Why not? Just give it a try! Lock yourselves away, take all the time in the world, and don't return before you can send up the white smoke.' After six or seven weeks they had at least a theoretical solution. And then we noticed that 38 out of 40 people suddenly had developed a strong motivation because they themselves couldn't believe what was happening. In the meantime the goal has been reached and we are able to only pull the few components a product really needs out of the back end. We have already started to save a tremendous amount of development costs today and are again a big step ahead on our way to our major goal: that of a completely digitalized company that is maximally geared towards its customers."

Terrific! These are the very success stories about reaching milestones any corporation needs, especially with regard to stakeholder management. Finally, I would like to know how Kai personally focuses himself in daily life. "I'm always very focused when I think about what my motivation really is," he says. "I want to make things better for our customers. Allianz is already incredibly successful. So what else is there to change and do significantly better? Having fun at work is also important to me. It's spoiled for me whenever political issues, personal goals and interests are put ahead of the interests of customers and the company. But as long as I feel the focus is fully on the customer and we are improving things, I'm focused and motivated. For me, personal focus also has to do with the digestible bites. To divide that one major issue into many small steps. And to be able to say 'no', too. I also don't want to take myself too seriously but rather convince others with achievements, solutions, and successes. Everything else will just follow then."

Many small goals on the way to the big goal

That one big goal can never be reached in one giant step. I'm not telling you anything new here. Slicing is always the smart thing to do. Making little packages, defining subgoals, declaring many small goals on the way to the big goal and celebrating the achievement of each small goal – that's the real challenge. Kai Czeschlik called it "digestible bites". Once again in this chapter, this brings us to something that sounds much simpler than its practical implementation really is. First of all: Focusing on one goal and working on small goals doesn't contradict but rather complements each other. The big goal will always be the guiding star. With every little target, you'll need to be able to see whether it's a step on the way to the big goal or if you're already starting to distract yourself. Take enough time to sort that out. Remember the reward system in your brain: We all prefer to do things that feel good immediately. However, it would be much more purposeful to first attend to that which is frequently difficult but important and unfortunately really unpleasant. *Eat that frog* is the name of the principle invented by Brian Tracy. Figuratively speaking: First of all, eat that disgusting frog; the delicious things will follow. This provides us with more energy right away. For postponing unpleasant things will drain you of a lot of mental energy. Having accomplished something difficult will also create good feelings – yet not at once but only afterwards.

> We all prefer to do things that feel good immediately. However, it would be much more purposeful to first attend to that which is frequently difficult but important and unfortunately really unpleasant.

Our mind is very creative when it comes to inventing justifications, and it is receptive to excuses when it's really all about endorphins. For example, a sugar-loaded candy bar called "fitness bar" and supposedly containing "lots of vitamins" won't contribute to your goal of keeping up a healthy diet, maintaining your ideal weight and keeping you physically fit. The label "fitness" attached to the bar and all these vitamins just provide you with a convenient excuse to get a short endorphin kick created by all that sugar. In companies it works similar. There will always be many people – both inside and outside the company – who will come and try to sell you their favourite pastimes as something that serves your strategy and pays into your big goal. Look closely and keep a clear mind. And always be able to say no. Further below you will find more on the issue of prioritization.

If you're absolutely sure that a particular small goal is the logical next step to the big goal, then concentrate fully on it. The big goal never becomes invisible. For example, you have a poster in your office that reminds you of a screensaver, a wall paper on your smartphone. You can put small anchors that will remind you of your purpose and the epic stuff you want to achieve in the end everywhere. At the same time, there is no one who can only have the big goal in mind all the time. Big goals also have something intimidating. There is the risk that the challenge might paralyze you. During a mountain hike you wouldn't stare constantly at the summit either. But you would gaze at it every now and then, thinking: Wow, it'll be absolutely spectacular when I'm up there, enjoying the view! Then you would focus again on the next part of your way. If you came across a dangerous spot, say a narrow path with steep sides, you would need to fully concentrate on that passage. Any thought of the summit would now be out of place and even risky.

Slicing helps you personally to keep the focus while it is extremely important for your stakeholder management in your company. You personally will stay focused on what matters at the moment and on the next logical milestone. In stakeholder management, you work with success stories that result from achieving sub-goals. After all, it's not enough to only use the narrative of the big final goal. As wonderful as that story may sound, it is often still too far away for people. So what you do is keep

> It's important to understand that people are guided by narratives and not by numbers, data and facts.

spreading little success stories and put them in the context of the big goal. Kai Czeschlik spends a lot of time on that kind of storytelling. You will also find a whole chapter on communication in this book. It's important to understand that people are guided by narratives and not by numbers, data and facts. Of course, the measurable results must be the right ones. But that's what every organization expects anyway. Success stories about achieved goals are what keeps your stakeholders happy. Suspicion of just slapping yourselves on the back can be countered by openness, clarity and focus on the resulting learning. Tell facts in the form of stories and let your listeners know why you're telling them.

The tech giants of Silicon Valley are known for mastering the art of slicing. Steve Jobs had the vision of a phone with no buttons and a touch screen for every input that was supposed to be not only a telephone and MP3 player but also a camera, calendar, Internet browser and much more. Without working methods suitable to achieving the goal in small steps, Apple would hardly have managed to launch the smartphone. And today we would all have to do without our favorite toy … The best-known method of Silicon Valley, which you probably have at least heard about, is OKR. The abbreviation stands for *objectives and key results*. On the qualitative side there are the *objectives*, the (bigger) goals that answer the question: Where do we want to go? On the quantitative side there are the *key results*; they denote the individual measurable steps required to reach the overall goal. OKR has become famous as a working method of Google. But it's much older than Google and was already applied by Intel in the mid-1970s. Venture capitalist John Doerr introduced OKR to Google in 1999 when the company was just one year old. Since then, Google has worked with the method, and sometimes it is claimed to be the corporation's true secret of success, which does seems slightly exaggerated after all.

In my opinion, it's definitely worth taking a closer look at OKR, even if in the end you don't want to proceed strictly according to that method. This framework sharpens the corporate awareness of goal setting and goal achievement every single day. Frequently goals are either too specific or too unspecific. OKR is a systematic management process that helps to define the right goals, to find suitable sub-goals and to focus on them. Objectives are always ambitious and may largely be outside people's comfort zone. Key results, on the other hand, are always easy to measure and are evaluated at the end of each quarter. The nice thing about OKRs is that they're agile. Intermediate results are constantly measured and evaluated, and everything can be corrected at any time. What matters most is the question of what will increase the likelihood of reaching the big goal as quickly and directly as possible. Every action in the company is checked to see if it pays into the big goal. Of course you can also make such an approach your habit independently of OKR. At some point, it will become a part of you.

On the personal level, agility leads directly back to the art of soft focus. If you stay calm and relaxed and pursue your goals in a laid-back manner, you'll also find it easy to be agile and to keep adapting everything whenever it is necessary. Managers, who are characterized by the traditional goal achievement and long-term agreement of goals in companies, often still find this very hard to do. They want to keep everything under control and are reluctant to switch to the Zen mode once in a while, to just let things happen and then correct and readjust them if necessary. They might be worried that employees may consider this kind of leadership weakness. Frequently only time will tell if goals are too specific or too unspecific. There is no formula you could use to always calculate this in advance. As a car manufacturer, for example, I might say: We want to become a leading provider of electric mobility and battery technology. But perhaps that's already too specific. What if there is a sudden technological breakthrough in drive technology no one has expected? And that as a result the road won't any longer lead only to E-motors and batteries? In that case the less specific goal of becoming the number one future provider of individual mobility would be a better goal.

At a time when everything is complex and volatile, and technologies are developing at a tremendously fast pace, relaxed executives are clearly at an advantage. Don't let VUCA drive you crazy! The faster the world outside is turning, the calmer you should stay, the more balanced, just waiting and seeing how things are developing. In the Zen mode you expect anything without letting anything bog you down.

That way you won't get hurt if things do turn out differently than expected. You always go with the flow and never against it – as in the Asian martial arts. Because I find these qualities so important, for this book I also wanted to talk to someone who

> At a time when everything is complex and volatile, and technologies are developing at a tremendously fast pace, relaxed executives are clearly at an advantage.

has never had anything to do with the corporate world but who understands all the more about Zen and martial arts.

Getting there with mindfulness, focus and concentration

The Shaolin monks are world famous for having invented kung fu. They have long been teaching this martial art to us in the Western world. A less well-known fact is that the original Shaolin Monastery in China is also the nucleus of Zen. However, unlike today's Zen Buddhists, the Shaolin monks don't rely solely on meditation but also on physical exercises, such as breathing techniques or even martial arts. Asian martial arts have always been a way to be fully in the presence and focused on the moment. That focus is much more important for success than any single combat technique. Basically, kung fu is not about fighting, it's about lifestyle. Controlling the mind and mastering the body with the mind is the objective. When fighting, Shaolin monks don't win because of physical strength but because of their mind, awareness and mental powers. That's what fascinates me about the Shaolin monks – and I very much look forward to my conversation with a representative of that principle.

Shaolin Master Yuan Lu has been living and teaching in Germany for 12 years. He runs a Shaolin centre in Schorndorf, in the State of Baden-Württemberg. We meet on a hot summer weekend. My wife has accompanied me to Schorndorf, and the three of us look for a shady spot embedded in nature. From here we have a breathtaking view over a picturesque valley. Yuan Lu's orange robe glows as brightly as the sun. He gives my wife and me a bottle of water for a gift. The label on the bottle reads: "Flower of life – love and gratitude." What a wonderful start! I thank Yuan Lu for the water and ask him for a short description of himself. It is neither the first nor the last time he shows his subtle and very warm smile. Then he says, "I grew up in China and went to the Shaolin temple 23 years ago to experience and learn the Shaolin arts at the monastery. All in all, I lived in the monastery for nine years and underwent hard training there. That mental and physical education has changed my life. I'm proud of what I've learned. My life was not easy. But what I learned has helped me to master every challenge along the road and to finally make a life for myself in Germany. Now I'm here enjoying my life, the peacefulness, my friends and being together with everyone I encounter in everyday life."

Yuan Lu radiates an incredible serenity while speaking. I explain to him that in the end we're doing a business book here – not an ordinary book but rather one that is about the people in corporations and the mindsets that make them achieve big goals. I also tell him a bit about the fact that today many companies want to practice more humanity and achieve their goals on the basis of appreciation. They try to get employees involved and help them focus even when they are flooded with all kinds of information every day. Therefore, I think, you can no longer separate your individual thinking from your attitude towards business. One will automatically affect the other. That's why leaders can learn something from those who are, so to speak, experts in mindfulness. So, first of all, I am interested in what mindfulness, what focus means to Yuan Lu personally.

"Mindfulness in the here and now will shape your future," Yuan Lu says. "We need to be mindful in everything we do now: the way we think, what we do, how we deal with people and things. The current moment is crucial for the future. The future will reflect everything we think, how we talk and interact with each other right now. That's what I think." I want to know why it is so important to focus while doing so. Can't I just do everything at the same time? "No, I can't," Yuan Lu says. "There is energy, there is the mind, and there's the body. I can invest 100 per cent of energy only into one thought at a time. That thought with that energy will then go into your body and into the outside world. We can reach our goals with that one thought that is filled with energy. Otherwise we always have just 80 per cent or 70 per cent or even less. Then we waste energy. In the end, that will result in mistakes. The Shaolin monks have this saying that 'We always give our best in what we're doing right now.' That's very important."

> I can invest 100 per cent of my energy only into one thought at a time.

Do the Shaolin Monks themselves achieve their goals by being mindful in any given moment and with the focus always on only one thing? "Yes, because that applies at any moment and in every area. We can only succeed if we're focused enough. Success is the result of a high degree of concentration, of mental training. Of course we also act, we can't just talk; we have to do a lot more than that. Only by doing can we build the future and improve things for the future." That makes sense. Actions are what matters in the end. But focus and concentration are at the beginning of the chain. It interests me how Yuan Lu personally focuses on something. "In every move, in everything I'm doing right now,

I go right into my every thought," he explains. Well, that sounds easy, and yet it is probably something you really need to master! Is there anything else? "I always give my best," Yuan Lu says. And I sense that when he says "always", he means always. "I also don't give up that quickly either," Yuan Lu continues. "I believe that our thoughts are stronger than our bodies. If our thoughts are powerful enough, our body will do what we're thinking."

In my opinion, what Yuan Lu has said so far can be transferred very well to daily business. Each one of us has only one mind and one body. People in business are constantly overtaxing themselves because they do a thousand things at the same time and think everything was equally important. Then there's always a new project that is absolutely essential, and then this and that and the other. It never stops. Work, work, work until all the energy has been drained from mind and body. Instead of focusing their energy on one thing and making it good, they pour their energy into far too many things simultaneously. Nodding, Yuan Lu says, "I agree. If you have too many projects, it can't work. Every project,

> Everyone knows that if you want to do pushups, you do pushups. You can't jump at the same time; that won't work.

every thing we want to be successful requires the necessary energy and mental concentration. If we always do a lot of things at once, we are constantly distracted. Our thoughts are here and sometimes there and sometimes somewhere else. But when we have three things on our mind at the same time, then all three will fail in the end. Everybody knows that when it comes to physical exercises. Everyone knows that if you want to do pushups, you do pushups. You can't jump at the same time; that won't work."

But when it comes to our thoughts, we believe simultaneity can work. Yet your thoughts go into your body and into the material world, as Yuan Lu has already explained. "There's a tension between body and mind," he explains. "If we want to exercise our stomach muscles, we also focus our thoughts on our stomach. This is the only way the exercise will work. It's the same with a project. Of course it's always better for the boss at the top when 10 or 20 people, instead of just one person, are doing something. That saves time and money. But in the end, quality is jeopardized and the human existence is threatened. Everything breaks down and we have nothing left." Many managers think: More is more. Yuan Lu shakes his head. "That's a bad idea. I'm good at Shaolin. But I can't be good at everything. I'm good at what I'm concentrating on. Because everything needs experience and the time to develop and grow. You can't be successful in many things at the same time."

Okay, if my readers now say, That's true, that makes sense to me, I want to focus more: Where should they start? "Definitely at home and not at the office," Yuan Lu suggests. "These days parents are talking to their children but nothing happens, the children don't respond. That's because the children's full attention is just not there. Sometimes parents don't even look the children in the eye while talking to them. That's just an example. You should always be mindful in everyday life: who you are talking to, how and about what. It's best to keep asking myself all day long: What am I doing right now? What's my goal? That question is like a tool. You should always know what you're doing and why you're doing it. That's how mindfulness comes into play. Then things can develop. At some point the concentration keeps getting better and better and the future becomes clearer."

I wonder why there are not more people who are taking that road. Yuan Lu has seen how many people feel pressured and are unhappy today, even his own students. The master is more than happy to help them, but everyone must change their way of thinking and their focus themselves. For the monk, contentment is the key. We often expect way too much. And Yuan Lu is convinced that the more we expect, the worse the result will be. "We can be happy to be here and now," he says in conclusion. "Enjoy our thoughts, our body, the moment. Just like we're sitting here right now. We meet at this beautiful place, sit here, relaxed, do an interview. That's really a wonderful moment. We're enjoying what's happening right now, and that's more important than what's going to happen later." I totally agree with him. Contentment in every moment and gratitude for what we have. Yuan Lu nods. "Gratitude, yes, that, too, is important."

Focus and concentration in daily practice

During my wonderful conversation with the Shaolin monk Yuan Lu, the way he manages to be focused at all times particularly impressed me. His advice is to practice mindfulness and concentration in practically every minute of your life. Why is that so important? After all, focusing on major, rewarding goals and useful sub-goals or milestones is demanding enough. There is always the need to set priorities and not to want too much at once. But what really distracts us are the topics at the micro level: the phone, that email, the assistant who comes in with a request for a very urgent appointment that requires your immediate decision, the employee who is knocking on at your door with a question, the works councilor with the suggestion to have lunch together in the canteen. Today, frequently hundreds of people vie for our attention, all at the same time. Of course, everyone is pursuing their own goals. Imagine you're surrounded by inboxes into which everybody is constantly throwing something. You have no chance to devote yourself to all these matters. Before you pay attention to the last issue, the day will be over and the boxes will be full again. Are you helplessly at the mercy of this? No, you're not.

You could make yourself, your thoughts and your goals your highest priority. And you could use defense techniques. Always remember that it's not primarily the others who want to take you by surprise, but rather the reward system in your own brains. Retrieved mails, pling, pling – great! Red badge gone, done – great! Completed annoying conversation, can strike it off – great! Avoid it and protect yourself and your focus. From now on, check your mails only manually, at fixed times and never first thing in the morning. Turn off all badges and notifications on your smartphone. It can be done – simply by changing the settings. Decide for yourself when to check your voicemails and WhatsApp messages, and don't be lured by previews on the lock screen. Do without a smartwatch; nobody needs it. If you really want one, then set it so it won't not bother you all the time. If you're working on texts and concepts, put Word in full-screen mode. Don't let anything pop up on your computer screen that has nothing to do with your current work. Refrain from spontaneous visits to social media. Before you log into Facebook, LinkedIn or Xing, ask yourself: What do I want here, what's the purpose? Then focus exclusively on that purpose. If you want to fully concentrate on something, put the smartphone in flight mode. I often even turn off my Wi-Fi! My motto is: I'm the one in control here, not the others.

Me-time is indispensable. My office has glass walls through which all employees can see me constantly. But when a red light is on and I wear my noise-canceling headphone on, everyone knows: no access! Set rules like these with your workers and insist that they be respected. What you do first thing in the morning is also very important. Instead of first processing emails – the biggest productivity killer ever – contemplate this: What do I want to do today to get closer to my big goal? Write it down and remember it during the day. What I've just mentioned as examples are many small measures. But in the end they make a big difference. The better you manage to eliminate distractions, the more focus you will have. It has been scientifically proven that it takes at least seven minutes after each disturbance to regain the level of concentration you had before. Seven minutes! Imagine you were distracted by some trifle matter every five minutes. Then you would never be completely focused!

> It has been scientifically proven that it takes at least seven minutes after each disturbance to regain the level of concentration you had before.

If I may summarize and deepen what's important in this chapter on focus, both in terms of the company and your own personal clarity and focus, then it is these five very simple steps:

1. **Brainstorming:** Which goals are important or could be worthwhile?
2. **Setting priorities:** What is the one goal and what are the three main sub-goals?
3. **Communicating:** Who are my stakeholders and what information do they need?
4. **Fending off:** What distracts me from the goal and how do I block this distraction?
5. **Staying tuned:** What gives me energy on the way and keeps my level of motivation high?

Brainstorming means first collecting everything: goals "from the top", your own goals, the goals of others, corporate goals, personal goals. What's important for the company and your own purpose? You are slowly starting to sense what epic stuff means to you and what you support all the way. Make your goals big and long-term and don't limit yourself. Success starts in your mind! Epic stuff means to work a lot, to work long hours and to work with pleasure. What is a great fun factor for you? Also visualize while brainstorming. What does a goal look like and how does it feel? Whatever seems to be easy to reach and doesn't motivate you at all is not a big goal. Then, in the second step, start prioritizing.

In most companies the wrong priorities are set. Priorities are categorized as being either "high", "medium" or "low" – and in the end, almost everything is "high". Make a list of one to ten. No two things can have the same priority. If in doubt, compare in pairs until the ranking is correct. Define Number One, your one goal. And then delete everything that is Priority Four or lower.

> In most companies the wrong priorities are set. Priorities are categorized as being either "high", "medium" or "low" – and in the end, almost everything is "high".

Once you've set your one goal, you must communicate it. Formulate your story. Talk to all bosses and stakeholders. Ensure that there's alignment; align the arrows. Develop your defense strategy in the next step and implement it consistently. What could distract you and reduce your focus? Think of the many potential little distractions and how to turn them off. Sometimes it's not necessary to do anything right away. Some things are fun but not urgent. Here you need discipline. Skillful communication is important here, too. Don't just ignore inquiries but ask back, "Could we discuss that in two hours instead of right now?" or, "Can we postpone that till next week?" Delegate as much as possible. Always be pleasant and maintain human contact.

Once you have started sorting out things consistently and focusing better, you may be surprised how well it works. In addition to the agreements you explicitly make with others, you will also benefit from a certain learning effect. If people know you're always available and approachable, they will also make use of it. If, on the other hand, they know that you concentrate on work and they should have a good reason for disturbing you, they will be prepared for that. You will again and again need willpower. Specially in the last and crucial step, which is about staying tuned and persevering. Stay on course, keep an eye on your goal and don't accept any excuses. At the same time, stay relaxed and never pursue your goal doggedly. Reward yourself from time to time. Make sure you stay motivated. The better you know your personal motivators, the better you can use them to keep up your spirits even if you experience setbacks, which are inevitable. Once you have managed to do that for yourself, turn to those around you. You are starting to positively influence the culture in your team and your company. You are turning it into a suitable breeding ground for epic stuff. That's what the next chapter is all about.

Chapter 4

What Everybody Is Striving for: The Culture that Makes Great Things Possible

"As a first rough concept for our new website, I already kind of like it," Sarah said, looking around. Her whole team was there. Sarah looked at tense faces that relaxed after this restrained praise from their boss. Some of the participants in the meeting even smiled softly. After all, what Sarah had just described as a "rough concept" was the result of several weeks of intensive team work. Sarah made a stern face. "But there's still something missing here completely, folks," the manager continued. She had been Head of Digital Communications in a traditional corporation for the past eighteen months. Suddenly the faces looked stressed again. "What I miss is the integration of our three most important company values. After all, these values define our corporate culture. And everyone who visits our website should see right away what our culture is." The tension in the room now gave way to utter perplexity. Everybody stared at Sarah. There was an unpleasant silence.

"Our three most important values, right," Mark said just in time before the silence became unbearable. "We should definitely integrate the culture. After all, our values were first defined last year. By that management consulting firm, what was its name again?" – "Emil Zenker, I think," Helen said. "Didn't they call themselves Baltimore Consulting or something like that?" Kevin thought out loud. – "Detroit. I'm sure it was Detroit!" Peter said. "Detroit and Touch." – "But they're our accountants." – "Oh, I thought they were taking care of our culture." – "It doesn't matter who it was," Mark said, ending the brief discussion. Sarah stared at him with a piercing look. "Anyway, that was initiated from the top, remember? The board wanted a culture. And then it developed one with the consultants. They defined our three most important values. And after that, we all underwent that training." – Sarah took a deep breath and exhaled slowly again. "Mark," she finally said in a calm voice. "If you remember the process so well, you could list our three most important values for everyone here in the room again."

Tiny beads of sweat appeared on Mark's forehead. "Well … our three most important values were … and still are … sustainability, customer focus and … um … profitability?" – "Sustainability will never come first!" Kevin protested. "Not with that conservative CEO." – "But profitability isn't correct either." Helen shook her head. "You don't define culture as being profitable. Either you are or you aren't." – "Tradition, innovation, perfection!" Peter shouted into the room as if he had found the solution to a difficult mathematical problem. – "That was the headline of one of our ads, Peter. But these are not our values." – "Wasn't there something about courage?" – "Hey, we're not boy scouts!" – "But quality was one of the three values. I'm absolutely sure. It was quality!" – "Stop it!" Sarah raised both hands. "I can't believe that none of you knows our three most important values," she said, frowning. Mark secretly wished he'd kept his mouth shut instead of adopting the role of the spokesman for the other team members. But now that he was the spokesman, he wanted to finish his part, too. "Please, Sarah," he began softly. "Would you please tell us again what our three most important values are?" Sarah swallowed hard. She suddenly turned pale. "Well, people, actually I'm no longer one hundred per cent sure myself anymore." She opened her laptop. "But I know exactly where I put the presentation … just a moment … I'll have it in a minute …"

Okay, I admit: What you just read is, for once, not a scenario I ever witnessed. That scenario is fictional. After all, exaggerations are good eye-openers. If you know the corporate world well, however, you might have noticed that I only slightly exaggerated everything. And that I stayed close to reality. I couldn't tell you in how many companies I witnessed a similar approach to culture.

It can happen that out of the blue, a management will think it's time to take care of company culture. Together with a consulting firm, it will then define what the culture should exactly be for the time being. The following process typically yields three to five core values that are as interchangeable as the heads of electric toothbrushes. The management then hires an agency that is to beautify the results. It initiates an internal communication process. There will be training courses for a year, in which the culture is to be conveyed across the board. Too bad that three weeks later the participants of such training courses will already have forgotten everything – except maybe how good or bad the food was and who was gossiping about whom. Having learned something is just not the same as having lived something. But can culture really be prescribed like valerian for sleep disorders? And what exactly is culture in a company anyway?

Culture is a breeding ground for everything a company can achieve. If I want to plant a tree that will grow tall and bear lots of fruit, then I need the right soil. It seems so obvious that you hardly ever think about it. The selection of the seedling and the planting process seem more important than soil analysis. It's similar with company culture. It's the basis for everything and at the same time always a given in any company. It doesn't matter whether it's reflected or

> Culture is a breeding ground for everything a company can achieve.

not. Yet the question is: Is there a positive culture? Is the soil good? Only a positive culture can be the breeding ground for big goals. The culture either fits in with the goals a company wants to achieve or it doesn't. In that sense, there's no right or wrong culture. Everything depends on the goals. In agriculture, there is no good or bad soil per se. It depends on what I want to plant. A rich soil for an orchard is not automatically just as good a ground for grain.

Anyone who pursues a major goal – no matter what that goal may be – will always need a culture that will serve that purpose. And if that culture doesn't exist yet, it's necessary to change the existing culture accordingly. This is not a new idea. Even within the context of change management, people like to talk about "cultural change" in the company. But cultural change can't be produced by management. Seeking to bring about cultural change by having a consulting firm designate interchangeable, diffuse values by making armchair decisions, and then teach them like compliance rules in training courses? That's a waste of time and money. Every individual who joins a new company will influence its culture. As does any new team member. Anyone who enters a room. Culture is based on people – and simultaneously has an effect on them. It's a constant cycle. Can you, in your leadership role, therefore shape the culture in your environment? Not only can you do it, you *are* doing it – every single day. The first step is to consciously do that which is subconscious. Cultural change begins on a small scale, with very concrete measures. How exactly these may look is explained in this chapter. The more conscious and effective you are, the more culture in your area of activity will become the breeding ground for great things.

The appropriate culture as a breeding ground for big goals

When it comes to culture, there are basically two types of leaders: One type of manager doesn't care about culture as an issue. He wants to concentrate on enforcing his agenda. In his opinion, culture is something for wimps. The other type is a real leader; she is aware of the importance of culture and loves to talk about this topic. She also likes to talk about values, empathy and the need to get all the people in the company involved. But if asked what exactly that means in concrete terms and how to build a positive culture, she will quickly be at the end of her wits. The first type of manager doesn't consider culture to be important. The second type considers it extremely important without knowing how to establish it. Of course that's a bit of a stereotype. You also have exceptions to the rule: managers who are outstanding role models, consciously shaping the culture in their environment. But on the whole, this is the situation I keep seeing. If I stick to the image of culture as a breeding ground, this situation will explain itself quite simply. Where the soil is good, I don't need to worry too much about soil quality. Instead I can just sow and harvest. In that sense, the first type doesn't automatically do anything wrong. But if the ground could be better, I could reap even more if I took better care of the ground. Maybe the soil quality is already being jeopardized; perhaps it will even be exhausted soon. Then I must immediately tend to the soil. The second type of manager is aware of that fact, yet she has dealt so little with soil qualities that she has no idea where to start.

Either way, to many leaders, culture is a book of seven seals. That is understandable from a human point of view. We usually don't prioritize any issue that we take for granted. And culture is always there as a matter of course. For a lecture given to German executives, an Indian top manager was once asked to talk a little about what he appreciated in Germany as a business location. The top manager started his lecture on legal security. He praised the German legal system to the skies. The executives listened, perplexed and surprised. For them, the issue of legal security had no part whatsoever in the discussion about Germany as a business location. We enjoy legal security anyway, right? So who really thinks about being able to sue their business partners for performance? Or that everyone is equal before the law? That employees are protected against being fired? Or that you can't circumvent environmental protection by bribing officials? The German managers who had assembled for the lecture took the whole legal framework for granted. For the Indian manager, however, German legal security was something very special and valuable.

Changing the culture in a positive way means, in a first step, consciously dealing with something that's already there. Many people don't think of culture for the very reason that is seems to be a natural given. So if you want to do epic stuff, you should first decide to pay attention to the issue of culture. Culture changes the results. Anyone who influences culture in a positive way creates the preconditions for better results. At this point, that's just a thesis. Later in this chapter you will find examples that show how powerful culture really is. Once you're aware of the culture, you will remember that everyone in the business, not just senior management and leaders, is constantly having an influence on company culture. Both for the better and for the worse – always with regard to what goal you have set yourself.

> Culture changes the results. Anyone who influences culture in a positive way creates the preconditions for better results.

You're probably familiar with the following phenomenon: A person enters a room – and immediately the atmosphere changes. Sometimes just a bit, sometimes substantially. A person with a radiant face and a good mood will immediately lift the spirits. Another individual, who is in a really foul mood, will drag everybody else down by just standing in the door. He or she doesn't even need to say a single word. There you have culture! Culture is permanently exposed to human influences and is constantly changing. Most people who contribute to a culture do so unknowingly. An applicant comes into the room, and everyone immediately thinks, "She fits into our company." In other words: She suits our culture. Another candidate enters, and everyone thinks, "He doesn't fit in." Afterwards, everybody comes up with rational arguments for hours on why she fits in and he doesn't. But actually that was already obvious from the very start. Culture has to do with resonance, with what someone is all about. And only secondarily with what they say or do. The great opportunity for you as a leader is that you consciously, permanently and systematically influence what everyone has been subconsciously influencing all along.

> **Culture has to do with resonance, with what someone is all about.**

What's more, you make culture the most important issue everyone works on together and everyone develops further together. Ideally, no single team member will then continue to subconsciously influence the culture of your company. Instead all of you will develop your positive culture together. And you, as their leader, are the guardian of your culture.

That requires common ground for you and your employees. At first, everyone will often define culture differently. Certainly you mean well by defining values. But as long as you all only come up with abstract terms, you won't see much progress. What does "sustainability" mean in concrete terms? Or "quality" – how does it show? Or "innovation" – what exactly is that? You should make things more concrete. Get to know each other and what is important to you better – because that's exactly what "values" are. Ask yourself: What's important to all of us? And more specifically: How do we want to deal with each other? In practical life, at your daily work, for instance during meetings. What rules apply then? What dos and don'ts? How do we want to communicate with each other? How do we deal with rumors? What's our language? How do we dress? What do we consider appropriate behaviour towards our customers and partners? At the end of the day, working on improving your

> **And you, as their leader, are the guardian of your culture.**

culture means coordinating and implementing many seemingly trivial details. *Details matter.* More about that later in this chapter.

When I founded my own company, the focus was on culture right from the start. I drew a pyramid with the term "culture", which was the basis for everything. Purpose, vision, strategy, and implementation are all based on that and on the corresponding values. The results are listed at the top of the pyramid. The culture forms the basis of everything. It's the pedestal. The foundation. My first coworkers and I already asked ourselves: What kind of culture do we want and need? We can achieve great goals together – what does our day-to-day work life look like? How do we deal with each other so that we can reach our goals with ease and joy? And one more thing was clear: We're moving forward with agility. We can always question everything over and over again and completely change it if necessary. Everything but our culture!

> Only because our culture is as it is, our outcomes are the way they are.

Culture as a supporting foundation requires continuity and permanent, careful development. We are constantly working on our culture, developing it together as a team. The founder is something like the guardian of culture in the interest of the entire team. In that sense, culture is the most important thing for us. It's about our identity. All results are ultimately based on our culture. Only because our culture is as it is, our outcomes are the way they are.

Now you may say: When founding a new company, a start-up, that's easy; there's this spirit of optimism and everyone is still in the mood to deal with such issues. Nothing is as complicated and historically evolved – not to say stuck – as in mature companies. You could say that, but it's not true. In the end it doesn't matter whether your organization is 5, 50 or 150 years old. You can start working more specifically on your culture everywhere – in the core team, in larger teams, and throughout the organization. A positive culture, which is still on a small scale, can always be expanded into a large culture. Of course you can find many subcultures in large organizations. The marketing department will have a different culture than the legal department. Each team needs its own culture. At the same time, there is the common culture of the company. If culture is like a breeding ground, then its soil consists of different layers. All layers should be healthy and contain water. The small plants get their water from the top layers, while the tall trees are supplied with water by the deeper layers. The gardener always watches where the water is flowing to.

A culture of trust attracts and thrills people

In Munich I have an appointment with an entrepreneur who is familiar with both cultural perspectives – that of the start-up and that of the grown company. Walter Gunz, born in 1946, founded the first Media Markt together with three business partners in 1979. When he left the executive board 20 years later, Media Markt was one of the world's largest consumer electronics retail chains. Today's Media Markt Saturn Retail Group employs around 62,000 people and generates more than € 21 billion annually. Our chief of staff, Sonja Weber, accompanies me on a hot summer day to the crowded gardens of an Italian restaurant to meet Walter Gunz. The thermometer refuses to stop at 35° C today. We're all the more pleased when we and our interviewee find an empty spot under a tall chestnut tree, probably the coolest spot you can find anywhere in Munich today. At first glance we had noticed only sunny spots outdoors and already braced ourselves for a literally heated discussion. Now we enjoy the gorgeous weather under the chestnut tree and start by ordering Aperol Spritz – the perfect drink for the season. We clink glasses; then I ask Walter Gunz to start by telling me a bit about himself first.

"It's not easy to talk about myself," admits the dyed-in-the-wool entrepreneur with a degree in philosophy, who started his business career at Karstadt in the 1970s. But Walter Gunz wants to tell uns one thing from his childhood and youth here in Munich, where he grew up with his mother: "I didn't do well in school. At secondary school I usually stood out for doing stupid things. And my teachers always made me feel like an idiot. Later in life that motivated me to seek freedom. These negative experiences in school were a kind of inspiration for me. Freedom became the central theme of my life. And that's how I really found freedom at work. It was never just about my individual freedom. Because I was free, I could trust other people. Trust and recognition were the most important elements for me at the company. Since I had always been made to look like an idiot at school, I knew what it felt like. I didn't want people who worked with me to ever feel not appreciated enough. They should be recognized and appreciated. But that was because of my freedom; it came from my heart."

That brings us straight to the topic of culture. Today everyone knows the logo of Media Markt. I want to know what vision Walter Gunz had at the beginning. How he managed culturally to build something people want to be part of and want to turn into something great together. "The most important thing is never to rise above the others," Walter Gunz says without thinking twice. "It's crucial to always talk to people on an equal footing. That's the precondition. Then it's love." Love? What does an entrepreneur mean by that? "You have to love what you're doing. Your company, the people you work with, your customers and suppliers. When I put my heart into something, then I do it right. If I'm motivated by money, success or prestige, things will go wrong. That's how it was with me from the start. I have this story: I quit Karstadt, where I was already in charge of consumer electronics, because there were too many rules, too many inspectors, too much restriction for my liking. After six months I met with my old team in a pub. They said to me, 'If you do anything again, we want to be part of it.' I remember driving home in the light grey BMW I had back then, thinking: What company would let me bring twelve people along? I'll have to start my own business! Then I can hire all twelve. Actually that was my motivation for founding my own company: to work again with the people I knew, people who trusted me."

So for Walter Gunz, a culture of trust in people was the basis for everything that would follow? "Yes, confidence, appreciation and love. Everybody wants to be loved and appreciated. *Recognized*, first of all. Recognition is a gift, something that doesn't originate from your ego but that falls to us from 'supra space', so to speak." The philosopher in Walter Gunz keeps showing. He truly is a thinker and a doer all rolled into one. Did the twelve members of his former team really follow him? "They did. Even though we had no money. Some of them had children but only one income, and even they, too, joined the first Media Markt. Of course, Karstadt tried everything to prevent that because they didn't want to lose the whole team. But the trust I had in them and they had in me was stronger than everything else."

Okay, thirteen people who have total confidence in each other. What a powerful tale! But how do you manage to preserve that culture? Media Markt grew grown rapidly in the following years. "The trick is to find people who will pass on the baton," Walter Gunz says. "People who value trust so much that they also pass it on to others. Plus there's something I described in my last book; I called it the 'loving gaze'. Everybody has a certain potential, absolutely everyone does. To look at people with love means to see their potential and then give them the opportunity to realize it. By having the confidence that somebody is able to do something, by entrusting something to them, that trust will make something come true. I appreciate and honour a person, telling him or her, 'Just do that now!' And then that person knows that someone believes in them. This belief in people is an initial spark that unleashes potential and will ultimately effect something great."

This is totally up my alley. That's what I believe in, too! And I can't wait to bring it across to people in companies. I can sense that Walter Gunz embodies what he says, that he lives and breathes it with every fiber of his body. And for him, culture also means to pass on the baton. "Or that torch," he adds. "I hand ten people a torch and ask them to carry the flame to whatever they're responsible for. Trust is something that lasts; that's why that flame can be passed on so well. Even today, CEOs I knew back then still call me on a regular basis. Trust is something that's durable, just like love. Unlike money and success, which are very, very transient. For me, today it's not crucial to have established a company of international standing that's represented by a red or blue box on every corner. Instead it gives me a sense of fulfillment when someone tells me, for instance: 'When you hired me as managing director for Bamberg, I thought it was great – but not as great as it really turned out to be.' I've heard people tell me things like that many times. And then I always say to myself: Walter, what more do you want?"

For Walter Gunz, culture is the passing on of a conviction and a certain kind of energy. That "loving look" at people – what does that mean to him? "It means to always be happy for your workers," he explains. "It always made me happy when someone made good money in my company. When Kaufhof unfortunately had bought the majority of our shares, one of the board members came to me, all upset about the salary of our branch manager in Rosenheim. The man was about to have a heart attack, saying, 'I'm the CEO of Kaufhof AG, and that guy in that lousy dump in Rosenheim makes just as much as me!' He couldn't believe it. I've always thought differently. Sharing is something I enjoy very much. Those who share with love can multiply their gains. That's my motto." Wonderful! By the way, we at FocusFirst think the same way. We're never concerned about money. It's not worth it.

The money will roll in automatically because we are who we are. Because we work together as if we were all good friends. "Exactly!" Walter Gunz agrees, adding, "I mean, everybody wants to be loved!" The co-founder of Media Markt managed to create an environment that people loved because they were appreciated and the management trusted them.

So what's the most important thing for an entrepreneur if you want to create that kind of positive culture? "To act," Walter Gunz says. "'Culture,' my professor used to say, comes from 'cult', and 'cult' comes from 'action'. Many people confuse culture with a feeling. But actually it's an act. Love and trust are acts as well. I *give* trust and I *get* trust. That may be accompanied by feelings, but the action is what's crucial. It's the same with love. Love can express itself in emotions, but the emotion isn't love yet. It

> Many people confuse culture with a feeling.

depends on the act. Yet to make sure that a certain spirit is passed on, that a flame is lit, that's also an act. Even one of the most important acts an entrepreneur can do."

At the end of our conversation I address the subject of gratitude. It's enormously important to me to be grateful. For Walter Gunz, gratitude is a key element in a company's culture, too. Gratitude to employees, customers, suppliers, simply to everyone. And what is the entrepreneur personally grateful for? "To be able to do things in freedom," Walter Gunz replies thoughtfully. "Because that's not something you can take for granted. There are countries in this world where you go to jail or even get your head chopped off if you stand up for freedom. So I'm grateful for the freedom I have."

The underestimated power of culture – and its pitfalls

The entrepreneur Walter Gunz has shown that, on the basis of a culture of trust and appreciation, a company of international standing can be created out of nowhere, so to speak. It was always obvious to the philosopher with an academic degree that interpersonal values are the best basis for lasting success. He has managed the feat not only of achieving goals of ambitious growth but also of making his employees happy. Working in freedom and with your own responsibilities, with ease and joy, together with people who really appreciate you and believe in great things – who wouldn't want that? While something like that is difficult to quantify, I may say that in most companies it's not like that yet. For twenty years or more, business gurus have been talking and writing about the "culture of trust". In change management, trust is traded as a "key factor". But how does that work in real businesses? Where do people work on a culture of trust and appreciation on a daily basis? How many teams have really reached a binding agreement about the basis of their cooperation? I totally agree with Walter Gunz: In the end, culture is just what you do, what you put into action. Everything else is nothing but fancy words. In almost every company today, you will find fancy words about values and culture. But what is actually practiced? Culture as a basis for everything is usually underestimated – sometimes until a painful learning experience lets the management realize the power of culture. Here is a story I was able to observe up close in a large company.

The initial situation was a classic change process: Two large departments in one corporation merged to become more efficient and save costs. This affected a total of 800 employees, and it was obvious that not everyone would be able to stay. The manager in charge – let's call him John – had to figure out whom to keep and whom to let go. As it's usually done when it comes to such unpleasant tasks, John hired a large international management consulting firm. It was known to make a clean sweep so as to make companies more efficient. The consulting firm conducted interviews with all 800 employees – following a questionnaire they had in their drawer for cases like this one. Afterwards, John sat down with the counselors. The method of the consulting firm was to divide the names of all employees into a quadrant system. John and his advisors gave the four boxes catchy names.

One quadrant was called "Stars" – these were the best workers John wanted to keep. A second quadrant was dedicated to the "Potentials", i. e. employees who still had the potential to grow. A third quadrant was called "Question Marks". The fourth and last quadrant was titled "Trash". Yes, that's right: *trash*. Garbage, waste, rejects. The names of the supposed underperformers without any potential for growth went into that box. John definitely wanted to let go of these employees. The result was as expected: The slide with the four quadrants was mailed all over the place, with more and more recipients listed in CC. And so the infamous slide circulated throughout the company. A shock. There was hardly any other topic people were talking about in the canteen: "In our company, management refers to people as *trash*!" The board slammed on the brakes. Not the employees listed in the fourth box were the first to be fired. But John. The board released him, effective immediately. At the same time, the board fired the consulting firm. Corporate culture was in shambles. It took a long time for the management to regain their employees' trust. Culture is the basis for everything. Here this showed in a negative and not a positive way.

Words are acts, too. In a positive culture, no one would come up with the idea of categorizing employees as *trash*. Of course people may make mistakes. That also includes using the wrong words to express something. The fatal thing about it was that nobody in John's company believed it to be just a small error. Instead, many people considered the slide to be evidence of the true attitude of the management and the actual culture that prevailed in the company. Culture has a far-reaching impact. Trust and appreciation also have impacts, as Walter Gunz showed us so impressively. Contempt for human beings, however, also has impacts.

It can pull a company under in no time. Once again the example of John shows: *You go first!* If you don't live up to your values as a leader, if you're not always careful of your words and actions, you won't be able to develop a positive culture. But isn't it unfair to be constantly under surveillance as a leader? Isn't it a mean thing if employees take every word you say too seriously? No, that's neither unfair nor mean. It's just part of your job.

> Culture has a far-reaching impact.

Growing together instead of stepping on each other's toes – that's culture. Doing something willingly that will have positive impacts. The motto is: Do good and talk about it. You've noticed that somebody did something really great last week? Of course you're going to tell others about it! A culture is spread and consolidated through storytelling. Strike gossip from your repertory and use positive, motivating success stories as a management tool. Every day provides countless small opportunities to do something for a positive culture. Even if it's only a simple "Thank you". A comment such as "Thank you for being so committed to this project" once in a while is also nice. Every daily practice, every little thing, is culture. Like a warm "Hello", too. I know corporations where even members of the same department don't say hello to each other in the hallway. They pass each other without even looking at each other. Things like that tell me more about the culture that is dominant in that company than a thirty-minute speech by the CEO about corporate values.

At the C-level, culture isn't a simple issue, anyway! That's a totally different story. For not a few old-school CEOs, the easiest thing to do would be to delegate the issue of culture to a consulting firm or specialized agency. Others are theoretically much further ahead but soon reach their limits when trying to implement their ideas. CEOs are under extremely heavy pressure and are expected to always deliver fast results. But cultural changes need time and patience. That's the crux of the matter. CDOs often have even less perseverance. Many digital bosses want to do away with antiquated customs and would like to turn the company upside down. Of course that's their job. There's a fine line, however, between expecting something and expecting too much of someone. I can relate to the dilemma on the C-level very well. Nevertheless, I tirelessly make the case for patience when it comes to working continuously on culture. A solid basis is particularly important in a rapidly changing environment. If everything is constantly changing, there should also be something everyone can rely on. And that's the culture! As Walter Gunz so aptly said, "Trust is something that's durable." Such cultural features as trust among people are durable. But in order to last, they also need enough time to grow.

I suggest that companies which have a conflict here adopt a two-pronged strategy. Be agile while patiently working on your culture. That's not necessarily a contradiction. The challenge is to separate the spheres. Here's an example: CDOs often love the term "error culture". They are brash enough to say to their employees, "Go ahead, make mistakes! That's no problem. Making mistakes means learning. Silicon Valley is doing it, too." That frequently overtaxes their employees totally. You can't turn the culture of a company in which everyone just tries to make no mistakes into a colourful playground after the model of Californian start-ups overnight. Imagine you're still working for the pharmaceutical or medical technology industry. Here, mistakes can cost lives – everyone has internalized that. Medication must not be contaminated under any circumstances, and pacemakers must be completely reliable. Yet now the spheres can be separated from each other: Does this pressure not to make any mistakes apply to all areas or only to certain sensitive areas? And couldn't you be a bit more adventurous in those areas that are not sensitive? Certainly you can't change anything here over-night, either. But it's possible to work on the culture as soon as you question old beliefs.

I keep hearing two objections to persistent work on a positive culture: First, there are different cultures all over the world. There-fore, it would be idle to work on "the" culture in a global corpo-ration. In addition, all efforts will become obsolete anyway as soon as the next major reorganization of the company comes around. Neither is true. A positive culture is not tied to ethnic or national boundaries. And it's precisely the aspect that will sur-vive all changes, the very aspect that makes it possible to get the people to come along on your journey over and over again. Of course there are certain differences between West Europeans and North Americans, East Asians and South Africans. But no-body in the world wants to be bullied, for example. Everyone wants to achieve something in life. Everybody would rather work in a nice environment than in a terrible one. At a certain level of prosperity, it's no longer only a question of money, either. And everywhere around the world, people feel better and more productive when they sense trust than when they're surrounded by distrust. These are global experi-ences.

> A positive culture is not tied to ethnic or national boundaries.

This is the perfect time to visit a global player whose brand products are loved by people around the world. I have an appoint-ment with Susann Kunz at Adidas in Herzogenaurach, where she works as Director Brand Strategy and Business Development for the sporting goods giant.

When teams work like football teams

Susann Kunz and I are sitting in the "Adi Dassler Room", a beautiful workshop room in a newly erected building on the premises of the headquarters of Adidas. A portrait of Adi Dassler that looks like it was drawn in chalk hangs on the wall. And antique tables create an exciting contrast in this new steel-and-glass building, a splendid atmosphere. I have known Susann for quite a while and am happy to meet her again today to talk about positive culture. As an introduction, I ask Susann what she personally considers a good culture. "That I can just be myself," she replies. "That I don't have to be perfect and may make mistakes as long as I keep inviting feedback from others and we work together to get better. All in all, I want to feel good and enjoy working where I work." So I want to know right away where Susann would start if she was in the position to create these conditions for others. Assuming she had just taken over a department with a staff of 100 and her job would be to ensure that those employees felt comfortable. And even assuming she couldn't lure anyone with a new vision or strategy because all that would still be in flux. Her job would just be to make sure that people wanted to stay aboard. What would Susann do?

"First I'd get to know people," Susann says. "Personal contact is very important. And by that I mean more than an open-door policy. I don't sit in my office with the door open, waiting for someone to stop by. Instead I go to the people myself, talk to them, make appointments. Ideally, I leave no one out even if there really are 100 or 200 employees. I also believe in common activities. For example, riding a bike to work together or doing yoga together every Friday morning. Various activities for smaller groups that will bring people together. And I mean as people, not just as colleagues." Is it actually that easy? Just be human, and you have a good culture? "I think it's easier than many people think,"

Susann says, convinced. "It's often made complicated to create trust with all sorts of approaches and formulas. At the end of the day, you just have to be human, let the others in the company be themselves and restrain yourself here and there. That's difficult in the context of a performance culture where everything is getting faster and faster. That's the real conflict. But here, too, humanity is the solution. Where people are allowed to just be humans, you may say, 'Hey, I'm not that well versed in this subject; could you please help me? By the way, if you ever have any questions about xy, please let me know and I'll try my best to help you with that.' That's exactly what will help the company in the end. Something like that works well – where everybody is open, people can be human and also admit if they have any weaknesses."

Wonderful. That also corresponds to my experience. Now I want to look at the top with Susann – not at the employees but rather those who might be supervisors. There are top managers, specially among global players, who say, "Culture? You should be making sales numbers, please!" Or others who may say, "You don't have to talk about culture. Everybody just be the way you are; that's fine." How would Susann respond to such top executives?

"Well, first of all, I'd say it's counterproductive not to talk about culture, because then a momentum will develop that may not match the values or goals of the company, because the people are still talking to each other anyway. And in that case culture will just develop in an uncoordinated way. If I can control something, I should make sure to steer it in a positive direction and not leave it to chance. Particularly if the company sets itself big goals. Secondly, I would say that the issue of positive corporate culture must be formally included in each employee's annual objectives as a point of evaluation and should be reviewed and continually improved over time. An important part of this is to hold the relevant executives accountable and to ensure that senior management periodically deals with and continues to promote that issue without compromise as a fixed item on the monthly agenda. In addition, it requires a body of non-executive staff to make concrete proposals, to create simple 3-to-6-month programmes and to implement them successfully. This will be about concrete things: What do we want to implement? How do we give feedback to each other? How do we deal with mistakes? At the same time we should always keep in mind where we want to go, what our North Star looks like."

Culture is a long journey and nothing that can be changed quickly overnight. After the first three to six months, it would then go deeper and more in detail. But does everyone feel like travelling? I would like to know how Susann deals with any resistance along the way. For example, with individuals who just don't want to participate. Or with structures in a group that make a further development of the culture a greater challenge, but which individuals stubbornly cling to.

> Culture is a long journey and nothing that can be changed quickly overnight.

"Basically, I take the time to talk to employees who might have a negative attitude on an equal footing and explain once again what our goals are, that we can only reach them together as a team, and how important the part that each individual plays in this is," Susann explains. "Everyone wants to be heard and taken seriously, and sometimes they may just get something off their back. Sure, there are people who always complain because they realize they get attention that way. In those cases it's necessary to set a clear framework and to let these individuals assume responsibility for themselves. To them I communicate unequivocally: 'Your part in this is very important and we need you, otherwise we won't get anywhere as a team.' As long as you have hierarchies – and you will find them in any organization – there will be difficulties, too. Ideally, you don't have any hierarchies at all. Here at Adidas, teams ideally collaborate as well as soccer teams. Everyone understands what their role and responsibilities are, be it the striker or the midfielder. Each player's role is as important as the next one, and each role has the same importance because it contributes equally to success. The coach brings the team forward and keeps developing it to make it better. Clearly, the coach sets the strategy, but the team organizes itself on the pitch, ultimately autonomously. The team is agile; that is, the striker will defend the team if the situation requires it. That's modern soccer – and that's a good guiding principle for us. Following this analogy, as a coach – that is, as a manager and coach – you are ideally more likely to ask questions and give impulses than just give directions: You ask, 'How did we play? How do you see the next game? What do we want to stand for? What does team spirit mean to us? What do we have to do to win?' I think that's a nice analogy."

Absolutely! Specially since in soccer, too, in the end, success is the result of a lot of detail work. Daily – or almost daily – training, practicing running, taking the ball, scoring, standard situations and so on. Everything with patience and just a bit better every day. Many little things will eventually make the difference between a good team and a top team. Sometimes it's just a small situation that will decide a soccer match. Finally, I want to know how Susan sees that. Not in terms of soccer, of course, but in terms of an environment where people like to work and do great things because they feel good. "A company doesn't need to spend all that much money to create a great environment," Susann says. "On the contrary, it's the little things that count the most. Celebrating birthdays, for example. A little ritual at the end of the week. Or I just telling someone, 'Good job!' That, for instance, doesn't cost anything at all."

Establishing and developing a positive culture at work

Yes, there are leaders who easily manage to create a positive culture while constantly developing it further. Those who are simply human, who don't take themselves too seriously – while knowing exactly when it's necessary to intervene. They know the right screws and in which direction to turn them. Justin is that kind of manager. (In real life he has a different name.) Justin was right in the middle of a complicated mega-merger that had the exchanges jubilating and the workforce howling. It was the classic situation: Nobody wanted to join forces with "the others". It was so nice and pleasant when we were still among ourselves! While top management was busy looking for synergies, many employees lost their composure. A head of department, for example, started projects without thinking twice just to close them again after a short time. Others went on sickleave for weeks. It was a cultural meltdown. The people had the rug pulled out from under their feet. They no longer felt secure; they were missing something they could trust and rely on. The performance was plummeting measurably.

In that challenging situation, Justin took over a team of 200 people in sales, with the help of whom he was expected to achieve successes again as quickly as possible. Justin knew just 20 of his new colleagues personally. It would have made sense to talk to everyone else in person, but there was no time. The pressure to succeed was just too great. Everyone Justin talked to was obviously afraid and felt insecure. Nobody had confidence in the future anymore. Justin noted that lack of transparency was a major issue. Again and again he heard someone ask the question: "What's going to happen now?" Unfortunately, Justin didn't have the answer either. The board was still sorting things out and provided only little information. In that difficult situation, Justin decided to be as honest and authentic as possible. He felt that a culture of openness was the solution. He said to his team members, "I know how difficult this time is for you. Can I change that? No. Do I know what will happen? No. But there's one thing we can change together: how we relate to this situation; how we deal with it. We can adopt a positive attitude. And we can be completely open to each other."

Justin then started to write an email to his team every Friday. In that email, he reviewed the past week. And he laid his knowledge as open as possible. He was always honest about what he knew and what he didn't know. Whenever he couldn't be as open as he would have liked to be because of anti-trust regulations, he referred to the contractual regulations and asked them to understand the restrictions he had to comply with. That allowed the team – and Justin – to build up trust again. Every member of the team started to have more self-confidence as well. In their meetings Justin kept asking, "How do we want to deal with this? What's our attitude?" And at the beginning of each meeting he asked, "How are you? How high is your energy level today?" An important cultural signal: You as human beings come first. Everything else follows. Soon a new culture emerged in the team. The majority of its members understood: We can talk about anything here. The team members also exchanged their views without Justin having to suggest it. It didn't take some of them long to say, "Hey, let's stop moaning and groaning; let's look at it as something that's positive." They took Justin as their role model. Of course no miracles happened in that team either. But Justin's team was productive again and could produce presentable numbers while other teams were still petrified.

> An important cultural signal:
> You as human beings come first.
> Everything else follows.

Justin's team clearly demonstrated what it takes to establish a positive culture in day-to-day operations. First of all, the leader has to follow this rule: Be authentic! *Walk your talk!* Then there are the numerous small screws. To get informed on a regular basis, for example. To disclose matters. To treat each other with appreciation. Culture must be tended to daily. Culture is like a beautiful garden that will quickly show signs of neglect. Leaders are used to talking about goals and expectations. Okay, that's nothing bad. Yet the *how* is frequently forgotten. How do we want to reach our goal as a team? That's the question of culture. And the actual basis for achieving any goals. Because now it's about daily working life, about what is lived experience. For instance, it's about whether it's okay to play with your smartphone during a meeting or not. Whether it's alright to get up and leave the room with the excuse: "Important call, sorry." Or if that's not okay. When you talk about that, you're talking about your culture.

Work out a framework of how you want to work together: *How we work*. By that I don't mean strict rules – you're adults, not schoolchildren. Think about what your values are and what you deduce from them. For example: "A respectful way of dealing with each other is to really listen to each other in meetings." For example, our agreement how we work at FocusFirst includes accepting responsibility, sharing our knowledge with each other and helping each other at all times. Such principles want to be lived daily. That requires feedback. The exchange about culture is something that's permanent and not something that's discussed once in a workshop and then ticked off. The timing is important as well. It won't do any good to start ten initiatives for the development of corporate culture at once and then do nothing for months. The order in which the measures are taken must also be considered. A good culture is the result of good strategic planning.

Very important for a positive culture: Ordering it top-down won't work. But exclusively bottom-up won't work either! That would be uncontrolled growth. The right balance is crucial: to initiate something from "the top" but also to use what is lived "at the bottom" and integrate it. Always talk to each other. Co-creation is hip. Find a consensus. As a leader you should know what kind of culture you would like to have. At the same time, you need to find out about the values of your team members and understand what's important to each individual. Talking about people you admire makes for a good workshop exercise. For instance, I think Frank Sinatra was a great guy. No matter how challenging a performance was, he always remained himself, with style, elegance, and a sense of humor. Someone may say she likes Lady Gaga. Or Shakira. Maybe she also admires Gandhi. Or Nelson Mandela. Or Mother Teresa. Never judge that but ask, "What is it you like about this personality? What exactly do you like about him/her? Is there something he/she has done in his/her life that you would do the same way?" This is how you learn about the values of your team member. You'll understand better what kind of culture this person wants and why. Then you may ask yourselves: How is that in our culture? Does it give room to these ideas? Or should we change something?

A good way to reach an agreement about the cultural basis is through surveys and voting processes. For example, you may brainstorm what the main principles of your daily cooperation should be. Then you take a vote. The result is a list of priorities. Then you delete everything from Prio 8 or Prio 10 or lower. Focus on this question: What is most important to us in our daily jobs? There is no right or wrong. Every company and every team is different. For one team, for example, the most important thing may be that everyone can completely trust one another and rely on each other. Another team may say: To us, autonomy is the crucial thing – that everyone takes full responsibility for their working area and that nobody just goes with the flow and lets his or her colleagues do their job. Working on the culture always means changing people's behaviour. You don't have to go through the trouble just to determine the status quo. Once you get results, communicate them! List them on posters, have them printed on your coffee cups – the sky's the limit. What's important is that everyone gets: This is how we want to treat each other. This is how we want to achieve our goals. And from now on, all of us will work on making it happen.

> Working on the culture always means changing people's behaviour.

Defining principles and values is always just the first step. The second step is: What exactly does that mean? The third step is constant reflection: How did we realize it today, this week, last month? What do we want to do even better, starting on Monday? Details count! That could also mean addressing unpleasant things directly. The sum of the details will create an environment in which the people you want to work with enjoy what they're doing and do a great job. An environment in which people know their own values and expectations as well as those of others and in which they are prepared to grow together. The more attractive your culture is to the people whose personalities it matches, the easier it will be to do epic stuff together. A positive culture is like a magnet for the very people you need. The next chapter is about how to get the right people excited about big goals. Dare to trust your personality and to live your values authentically. And work daily on a culture in which everybody works enthusiastically towards big goals.

> A positive culture is like a magnet for the very people you need.

Chapter 5

Your Team Is Larger Than You Think: Get Everyone Involved

"Hey, Tim!" Patrick called from a corner with a wildly sprawling ficus. Tim stopped in his tracks, turned around and grinned. The corridors of the corporate headquarters were so long and twisty that people would often pass their best buddies without noticing them. "How did your appointment with the CEO go?" Patrick asked. "A great plan, but no team and no money," Tim replied, grinning even wider. "The usual story," Patrick said dryly. Then he asked, "What miracle are you supposed to do?" Tim laughed. "To conjure up a web presence that is globally uniform." Patrick raised his eyebrows. "How much time did our CEO take to discuss the job with you? Ten minutes?" – "Fifteen." – "Then it must be really important to him!" – "Patrick, can you say right off the bet how many local websites we have right now?" – "19." – "As many as regional companies?" – "Exactly." – "And how well have the respective persons in charge been working together so far?" – "Not at all." – "So it can only get better." – "Looks like it." Patrick gave Tim a friendly tap on his shoulder, saying, "Well, if you're looking for a team now, I'm in." Tim beamed. "Great! I'll be able to put you to use. After all, you've been on our oil tanker longer and know it better than me. Do you have time this week? Then we could go to Wanda's Magical Coffee, have a cappuccino or two and take a look at the 19 websites on the notebook."

Two days later, Tim and Patrick sat in the small coffee bar diagonally opposite from the main entrance to the corporate tower.

They were looking at the monitor of Tim's notebook. "Every local website looks different," Tim said, shaking his head. "If they could, they'd probably even adapt our logo to their respective national colours." Patrick opened an email on his tablet. "Look at the number of visitors Linda has just sent us. Japan's traffic is crazy compared to all the others. The German site doesn't seem to interest anybody. Hardly any visitors." Tim looked thoughtful. "So we do already have something like best practice. We'll congratulate the Japanese and ask them to present for the others what they've done. But first of all we'll make a team out of all those internet tinkerers that are scattered all over the world! The dream team for our new global website." – "*Wanda's Magical Web Team*," Patrick said with a chuckle. "Without Wanda it wouldn't even sound bad: *The Magical Webteam*." – "Or how about the *New Web Crew*?" – "Sounds great! NWC for short. We'll create a really cool logo for the NWC. One that looks similar to the NFL. Just minus the football, of course, and maybe more international in design." Tim looked at Patrick. Patrick nodded. Tim finished his cappuccino. "The first step should be to get to know all future team members," he suggested. "And to get some kind of budget."

Four weeks later, all of the corporation's local employees who were in charge of the web met for a kick-off meeting in Kuala Lumpur. At the end of the two-day meeting, Tim distributed small pins with the inscription NWC – New Web Crew. Patrick's favorite graphic artist had created a logo that actually looked like a sports team. The pin had been produced by a manufacturer of promotional items for small change. The eyes of most team members from all over the world lit up when they put it on with pride. And they were excited about the past two days. For some of the web teams from different countries it had been the first business flight to another country. They were staying in a beautiful hotel. And they had already achieved really good results. The Japanese had given away their keys to success. But not only that. There was already a concept of how everyone could learn from each other in the future. Tim had suggested calls every other week, which everybody agreed with. Fortunately, the issue of the budget was also resolved. While Tim and Patrick were sitting in a taxi that took them to the airport, Tim was certain: Everyone will act in concert. "Just three days ago we didn't have a team yet but now we do," he said to Patrick. "It almost feels like we started a movement in the company," Patrick agreed. "We're doing epic stuff here!"

The website project, a summarized version of which is described in the above story, was actually realized in a corporation. The manager in charge – his name was not Tim – had a huge job to do without a team or a budget to start with. Perhaps you're familiar with a situation like that? In my observation, this constellation is the rule in the corporate world. And that's not surprising. Everything becomes agile, and the side effects can be quite challenging for executives. The relaxed old days are coming to an end. Instead of the management saying coolly, "Dear Project Manager, that's your new task; these are your twenty full-time equivalents, this is your – generous – budget, and this is what the approximate timeframe we would like to see looks like." Today, a CEO will stop by – as in Tim's case – and say something like that: "Re-create our web presence." That's all the information you'll get. If you protest, they will say, "Well, other people manage to do it, too!" In other words: Where you get the people and the money is your problem. At the top level, there's just no time to bother with details.

So what are your options? You can work until you burn out just to get your job done more or less single-handedly. Which is a very unhealthy idea. And one that is sure to fail even with the greatest self-sacrifice possible. Is there a smarter approach? Yes, there is! The good news is that today you always have the opportunity to form a team in any corporate. Even if your future team members don't know yet how lucky they are. Good networkers can almost always organize a budget as well. Even if it may require a bit of patience. Here, it all starts with the right mindset, too. You no longer think like a classical project leader that has to shoulder everything. Instead you think like an entrepreneur within the company, an *intrapreneur*. Entrepreneurs never tackle all topics themselves. Instead they organize the work, turning people into workers. You

> If you touch people emotionally, then you will quickly have a team. And it will be larger than you've initially expected.

do the same in the company. While doing so, your knowledge of the organization chart will be of little use to you – but knowing what motivates and thrills people and what they enjoy doing will be very helpful to you. If you touch people emotionally, then you will quickly have a team. And it will be larger than you've initially expected. All you have to do is recognize and activate it!

Involving people to create great things together

Today we are seeing a kind of hybrid age in established corporations. The old structures are still there, all those matrix, construction and process organizations left as a legacy by the management theory of the 20th century. Even Taylorism frequently still exists – according to which all expertise accumulates "at the top" like inside a bloated head and nobody "at the bottom" knows anything. After all, command and control are by no means everywhere a thing of the past. Even companies that present themselves to the outside as innovative are sometimes authoritarian. There's an alpha leader somewhere that everyone is afraid of. Yet people are starting to do things differently even within these old corporate structures. They are organizing themselves – within the given options – more and more often. This gives corporates their hybrid character. People are working in the old structures, for better or worse, while creating something new, being intrinsically motivated. In this hybrid age it's possible to get employees excited about epic things. Things that are not in their job description and for which they weren't hired – at least not officially. These things are not just fun for those involved but will also help the whole company on significantly. That's why they often inspire all stakeholders in the end.

The concept of *Working Out Loud* (WOL), as introduced by IT expert Bryce Williams in 2010, is a fine example of the changing mentality in large companies. The basic idea of WOL is to network across traditional organizational and hierarchical boundaries, share knowledge and learn together. Working Out Loud is a pun on the phrase "laughing out loud", and fun plays a key role in the concept. The point is to stop working stubbornly and doggedly in a company – and to start talking to as many others as possible about their work. The primary goal is to improve everybody's skills by permanently sharing knowledge. The idea is to depart from privileged knowledge. Everyone talks to everyone else about everything. Knowledge is there to be shared. And it no longer serves to position oneself or gain advantages over others. Bryce Williams has turned WOL into a method and a structured process that has created *communities of practice* in corporations.

More important than these circles and official learning groups is the mentality change that is behind it. Everyone can be inspired by *Working Out Loud* by simply talking to others in the company about their work as often as possible. Tell people the story that is behind what you're doing right now. And listen to others more often! Ask them what they're working on. Take an active interest in their work. And give ideas away generously. Instead of talking about the weather or soccer, Tim and Patrick talk about what they're working on even when they happen to meet in the hallway.

Just ask yourself how many times a day you talk to others about trivialities, and how much more useful you could spend that time sharing knowledge, ideas, and inspiration. Patrick likes to take the time to sit down with Tim so that Tim's project gets back on track. He knows that Tim would do the same for him. As is the case with effective networking, none of them is looking for a quick return. Nurturing relationships often pays off in the long run – just like generosity, which, by the way, is one of the core values of *Working Out Loud*.

As soon as you are suddenly faced with a major task, but without a team and possibly not even a budget, you will find out how good your relationship management has been lately. Have you maintained a friendly level with many people? Have you often exchanged ideas? Did you listen to others? Did you tell them if their work inspired you? And given them tips willingly? Did you show your co-workers that you appreciate them? For example, by buying them a cup of coffee, by giving someone a delicious bar of chocolate or – the healthier option – by inviting someone to exercise together in the evening? Did you have fun with those around you? Did you make people laugh? The more of the above applies, the easier you will get support for your task. You won't have to plead with anyone. People will take the time to contribute to your project even if they don't really have much time. They will just make your request their priority. Because we always make people we trust, who are open and appreciative and with whom we have fun on a regular basis, our priority.

Therefore chances are you will get a large and motivated team even if officially none or only a very small team is available. You may also question the term "team". In the old world – which may still be around for quite a while in the hybrid age – a team consists of people who are assigned to work together in a department or on a project. So there is the CRM team, the legal team, the team that works on a specific change project, the cleaning team, and so on. These are old, well-defined teams. In the new world your team includes all those who help you achieve your goals – perhaps for 40 hours or for half an hour a week. They may be your closest friends as well as people you've only met once in person and with whom you will only be in contact via Skype from then on. They may be people from all countries and nearly all hierarchical levels. They are simply everyone you can get excited about your issue. Even people who don't get paid for helping you but who do it solely because of the fun factor and the appreciation that they get out of it.

> In the new world your team includes all those who help you achieve your goals.

Getting everyone aboard even if no one reports to you

Martin Stork's mission is to get about 120,000 people around the world excited about digital transformation. He has only a small team in the classical sense of reporting directly to him. "Small but perfectly formed," as he puts it, "but sadly not sufficient, considering the long list of tasks and ideas." As Head of Workforce Enablement, Martin is in charge of the HR side of digital transformation at BASF. His job is to get everyone in the entire HR value chain – from employer branding to recruiting and onboarding to employee and leadership development – interested in the digital age. One of his tasks is to initiate a transformation in people's minds. He is to motivate employees to contribute their own ideas for digitizing the company. This is an exciting time for him and his job is a lot of fun, he assures me. Not least because he managed to expand his actual team to include other colleagues who, although they do not technically report to him, simply believe in the matter and therefore want to make a contribution. Martin's whole career was shaped by BASF. He joined the company 14 years ago as part of a dual degree academic course and then decided to stay. Apart from HR, he already worked in controlling and IT. We meet in "Speicher 7" in Mannheim, a stylish and very fancy hotel located in a former granary at the harbor. The bar we settle in has its own unique style and immediately reminds me of Indonesia. We enjoy a great view of the Rhine. You can discern the gigantic manufacturing plant of BASF in Ludwigshafen on the other side of the river.

For me, Martin is the prime example of a leader who keeps re-creating his own team. His job is to reach virtually all BASF employees. They are scattered all over the world, in countless areas and on many hierarchical levels. Apart from his small circle of closest associates, Martin has no authority over anyone. Everyone reports to other managers. Greatly committed to his job, Martin still does ingenious things with them. I frequently follow up on this via LinkedIn. Anyone who acts like Martin needs special qualities, mindsets and strategies for success. Sometimes they are not even strategies but simply creative and experimental approaches. It's not a child's play to get tens of thousands of employees in a corporation to find a status X better than the status quo and get involved in new situations. What exactly does Martin do to get his team members involved? How does he make sure that everyone is happy to deal with the digital future? That's what I want to find out first.

"For me, getting people involved first of all means understanding what digital transformation means to them," Martin explains. "That's the only way they can actively contribute. That means we make the topic tangible and comprehensible. Not only in theory but also in practice. We always rely heavily on experience. It's not enough if people in the seminar room undergo training. You must experience everything first hand. For this we use different formats, because everybody experiences things differently. We use barcamps, for instance." This is the design of an open event during which the participants first define the exact content themselves, then intensively exchange ideas and finally produce results together. "Exactly. Employees come together in a barcamp and work exclusively on their own ideas. On their *own* ideas! That's what makes the difference. At events like this, it's always great to see how people can show what great ideas they have and how they themselves can contribute to the digital transformation."

That's not necessarily the rule in a corporate. A lot of topics are still dictated by the top management. Not every leader dares to just let people do their own thing. "Yes, and that's why it's so great to experience the energy and dynamics that are in the air. It's simply fun. Of course the goal is also to get out of the silos and bring people together. The digital transformation can only happen if people work together, in networks and communities within the company. We are now breaking through the silos and creating cross-functional and cross-organizational teams. Recently we had a special barcamp where employees completely organized themselves and teamed up to develop their ideas. What was special about it was that this was later pitched in front of a jury, based on the model of 'Shark Tank'. The objective was to find a sponsor for every good project idea in the company. We had no idea what would come out of it. I think that with three out of five ideas, one sponsor immediately got up and offered their support. Everyone was happy to have space for their ideas and to get so much encouragement. That was really great."

Are there any other examples? "Yes, there are. In order to advance our employer's brand, we have already conducted several hackathons," Martin reports. "Students and young professionals, most of whom didn't yet know each other, came together to work 24 hours on the solution to a problem. And after those 24 hours they did present a solution that really blew us away." I think that really rocks! Goosebump moments like that are extremely important. Afterwards the people may be exhausted, but at the same time they also get new energy. It's similar to mountain climbing. Yet now I can imagine that some readers will say: Sounds great and really easy. But my own situation is totally different. I have a major project to accomplish and only get seven FTEs for it. But I would need at least 50 full-time equivalents of workforce. How am I supposed to swing that? I guess it would be best not to accept this mandate at all.

"Once in a while you just have to be courageous and go new ways," Martin says. "Actually the potential is always there in a large company. I think many organizations have no idea what skills they have in their own ranks. To take advantage of this potential, everyone should stop focusing only on their own silos. Instead, they should just take a look around to see who feels like doing what. As a result, people who have intrinsic motivation will approach the issues. They just want to get involved in a topic, and so they will somehow manage to spend part of their time on it. No matter who they report to. I think you have to start making that more visible. In other words, you should provide a platform for people and give them the opportunity to come together and work together on a specific theme. All this without asking how many FTEs someone has on paper. If I manage to inspire people and just convince them that something is a good thing, then a project will take off by itself."

Today, self-organization is everything when it comes to teams. Our conversation has convinced me of that once again. At the same time, you actually always need someone who will lead and inspire and motivate people. Finally, I would like to know from Martin what his personal approach is to inspire people. "Being inspired yourself is enormously important to me," he says, "and what inspires me most is to see what people can do together when they get the chance. That's why I also believe that one of any manager's tasks is to create the necessary freedom for that. Ultimately, then, as a leader, you inspire because of your authenticity. If people believe what you're saying at any given moment, and if they sense that you're really convinced of it, then you can move mountains. Plus you need trust and empowerment. That means you trust people and have the confidence that they really can make a difference. When people know why they're doing something, they will realize their full potential."

Connecting issues with emotions to keep people excited

Back to you: You have invested time, ideas, and appreciation in a network of helpful contacts. All that is still missing is that people also feel like working on your issue! Certain topics may seem more attractive than others at first sight. While one topic immediately sounds like fun, another one may sound dry. The purpose of one issue becomes immediately apparent – while it may yet have to be defined in another case. But whatever you plan to do: There are no boring topics. There are only boring wrappings! And if the purpose is clear to you, if you know exactly what your goal is and why you're about to reach that goal, then you can always make the purpose clear to others, too. It's like Christo's art: The world-famous artist turns all kinds of objects into pieces of art by wrapping them. Emotions are the most important thing about wrapping in any corporation. Emotions are often forgotten in business. You know that. Yet it's the human factor that will create the greatest intrinsic motivation to join your team.

> But whatever you plan to do:
> There are no boring topics.
> There are only boring wrappings!

I recall the time when a new CRM was to be introduced in a large corporation. Nobody felt like doing it. That was completely incomprehensible to me. In fact, CRM is an exciting thing! It's all about the relationship with the customer, so actually it's the most important thing in a company. As we took a closer look at the project and its start-up difficulties, we realized: You can hardly wrap anything as boringly as they did! The project name was a technocratic word and about as sexy as a DHL tracking number. No one could remember that name right away. The project description was not about the customer or about relationships – even though CRM is short for "customer relationship management" – but about the technical requirements for a possible new software. And about various potential IT suppliers, their advantages and disadvantages and so on. What overall impression was created? A complex, tricky IT project that would probably take forever, cause a lot of trouble and won't even pay off in the end. At any rate, the purpose of the whole project was not mentioned anywhere.

With our support, the project manager then rewrapped the project. His approach was to consider everything from the human perspective. The technology was ignored for the time being. Obviously you will need a lot of technology in the end; however, it's not an end in itself but should rather support what you really want to achieve. The project was now called "Smile", and the story line was that the focus of the project was to make customers smile. That may sound trivial at first, but it was the crucial mind shift. All of a sudden the focus was on the customers – how they feel, how they perceive the company. Now the purpose was also clear: to ensure that every contact with the company is a positive experience for the customer. Matching posters with smiling customers were then pinned on the walls. Those involved in the project later got buttons with the inscription "I make customers smile". The effect was incredible: A project nobody had wanted to do had become a project that almost created a hype in the company.

The question from the perspective of potential team members is always: Why should I care about this issue? Numbers, data and facts are only helpful to a certain extent. Emotion must always be part of it. I recall dry issues, such as compliance or operational safety. Stories helped to get people excited about these projects. Narratives that focused on the human aspect of the issue and charged it with emotions. After the team members had grasped how significant their work was regarding people's safety, they were almost as motivated as firefighters or paramedics. Instantly they knew that this wasn't about DIN regulations or any other legal requirements. Instead it was about protecting people from serious hazards and giving them the good feeling that they were safe at their workplace and that nothing could happen to them.

When it comes to issues that are hard to communicate, it can be helpful at times to link them to another issue that may not have anything to do with the contents of the first one. That will create a second, positive narrative that radiates back to the first issue. A great example of that was a global team that came together for a project and agreed from the outset that they would donate five per cent of their working time to the construction of a well in a village in Central Africa. In the end, the team members celebrated not only their successful project but also the unveiling of the well in the African village.

People come aboard because appreciation, recognition and joy attract them. They feel like working with interesting people on something meaningful. Unfortunately we live in times when many people find it difficult to keep up their focus – see Chapter 3. Distractions lurk on every corner. And whatever was the latest idea that thrilled us yesterday can bore us today – because someone has already come up with another idea. Specially with teams you have no direct control over, you may want to think about how to keep up the fire of enthusiasm over a longer period of time. After all, everyone can decide at any time to give your topic less priority again. Or join others in the business.

> People come aboard because appreciation, recognition and joy attract them.

A good motivator for the long haul is communication on a regular basis. People love to work together on meaningful things and to exchange facts and ideas, too. If meetings of all participants on a regular basis are too time-consuming, then at least arrange for virtual meetings at regular intervals via Skype or similar tools. Get used to turning on your webcam each time. It's important not to restructure everything but to leave space for spontaneity instead. Let people talk about their successes *and* their problems. Let them go wild and dare to present ideas that haven't really been developed yet. Of course milestones you have

> People love to work together on meaningful things and to exchange facts and ideas, too.

reached will be celebrated together. There are already unique ideas of how even virtual teams can celebrate together. For instance that everybody comes in a costume to a Skype call and has the same drink on their table. This is fun and will weld the team together. Periodical short keynotes written by guests – from other companies as well – who report on their experiences in similar projects is another nice idea that will also promote a culture of learning and sharing knowledge.

What I particularly love to use to connect or revitalize large teams that may be scattered at times is a *team connector* – something haptic, such as a pin, a badge or a ribbon only the team members have. This will make their sense of belonging to the team literally tangible. At one time there was this project for the digitization of logistics in a globally operating company that still operated very analogously at the time. The project was called "Conquer", probably because for most of the participants it really meant to conquer new territory. After an enthusiastic start, the project started to falter. It was hard for the project leader to reach any milestones. When we examined the situation with the project leader, it became clear that there was little sense of belonging and little intrinsic motivation among those involved, who were scattered around the world. Individuals had hardly received any appreciation for their pioneering role from which the entire company benefitted.

We then had these really nice wristbands made that had "Digital Hero" printed on them. The ribbons were available in two colours: dark blue and orange. Each local person in charge received a dark blue ribbon along with a thank-you letter from the project manager for the commitment they had shown this far. Included were 10 orange ribbons the person in charge could give to their team members as a token of appreciation for their commitment. The ribbons were sent to 45 countries, and the whole effort cost only € 900. The effect was huge. Even months later, teams from individual countries still posted group photos on LinkedIn that showed the team members with beaming faces, proudly presenting the ribbons on their arms. Sometimes it really is that easy! As soon as just a bit more emotion comes into play, connectedness becomes noticeable and there is recognition and appreciation, people will be motivated again. Okay, it's not always that easy. Creating or keeping a team can sometimes be extremely challenging.

Overcoming hurdles on the way to the team and consolidating trust

A medium-sized food manufacturer somewhere in rural Bavaria. After the takeover by a global corporation, the spirits of the workforce were low. The previous owner was already 80 years old and had no successor. That was why he sold the company. It required major modernizing measures. However, many of the employees were used to the situation. The low utilization of the production facilities caused long breaks during the conversion to other products. What also characterized the company was the pronounced formation of small groups. There were hostile feelings between the marketing department and the sales department, and they worked more against each other than with each other. The CRM had never worked properly, but the employees didn't seem to care. The new owner's management decided to boost short-term sales as there was a great deal of potential here. After that, the production was to be modernized. The first concrete step was the introduction of Salesforce. At the kick-off of the project the new CEO raved about the software: The CRM would be part of the global architecture of the company. Salesforce would make everything transparent and each individual's performance measurable. Mike, the project manager, who was standing next to her, nodded.

The manager and her project manager were facing 30 members of sales and marketing – strictly separated by department, sitting at different tables with gloomy faces, their arms folded across their chests. In the front, the project was presented passionately, explained in detail, made palatable. But it sounded as if Mike and his boss wanted to explain to five-year-olds how much more fun school was than playing with their friends all day long. Nobody wanted this project. On the contrary, many feared constant surveillance. They were used to the fact that the management didn't look at their results too closely.

In that challenging situation, Mike started one-on-one talks in a protected and confidential environment. He wanted to understand everyone's worries and concerns. Mike also let people blow off steam without contradicting or judging anything. That was a very important factor. Sometimes employees simply want someone who will listen to them. Someone may even have a grudge for years because of some trivial trifle. Once that individual gets the chance to talk about it and has someone who really listens to their complaint, differences can often be put aside. Just talking about it can have a positive effect. Incidentally, this insight is the basis of the conversation psychotherapy founded by Carl Rogers. The method of "active listening" developed by Rogers is also used in coaching and conflict mediation today.

Mike also did some kind of field research on the side. He spoke to everyone in the company, the former owner, customers and suppliers. He checked out every office, studied the website, looked at photos taken during company parties. All that helped him to resonate and not just look at the company on an abstract level but also develop a sense of what was going on here. This and the one-on-one interviews already created a bit more trust. In the end, Mike understood a significant connexion: Before the former boss had become negligent due to old age, he had led the company in an authoritarian manner, using pressure and threats. His reaction to any mistakes had always been to throw a temper tantrum. There had been a company culture of fear from which the staff now started to recover. Subconsciously, many workers seemed to fear that the new owner would bring pressure and stress back. Mike, however, seemed relaxed and empathic. Of course he strived for a better performance in the end. Yet he wanted to get everyone involved.

> Of course he strived for a better performance in the end. Yet he wanted to get everyone involved.

In the next step, Mike formed four workshop groups and asked them, "How do we want to work together in the future?" He was interested in the culture, the how-we-work. The employees realized that their wishes and ideas mattered. One wish was that they'd be praised for a change, instead of always being criticized. They also addressed supposedly little things, such as coming to meetings on time as an expression of respect for others. Slowly, Mike came closer to the people's emotions. The breakthrough was a workshop in which Mike asked them: What's your dream? What are your wishes for the future? At first only a few people opened up. Then more and more thawed out. In another workshop, Mike finally had them in the bag: Wouldn't the restart as part of a corporation – with everything that came with it – also provide an opportunity to finally work

> They no longer regarded transparency as something threatening. But as an expression of a new openness in personal interaction with each other.

and interact as they had always wanted to? Eight out of ten marketing and sales employees finally agreed. They no longer regarded transparency as something threatening. But as an expression of a new openness in personal interaction with each other.

What Mike has implemented here step by step can be called a *designing alliance*. In the beginning, the prerequisites for connecting people and aligning them to a goal had not been there. In that kind of situation it won't do any good to tout the subject or wrap it nicely. That won't lure anybody. Sometimes it's necessary to first build trust and dispose of old ballast. To win people is always the be-all and end-all. Sometimes the prospect of a great project with really good people is enough – and at other times you should start with a deeper perspective. Either way, the human factor is crucial for the team's success. At the end of the day – you can be sure – people would rather joyously do something meaningful than grouchily defend small personal liberties. Those are times they will then spend with Facebook or with gossiping next to the coffeemaker.

More and more leaders, regardless of their generation, know how to win the trust of all employees, inspire them and, together, aim for big goals. So does Klaus Straub, at the time we meet the CIO and Senior Vice President of Information Management at the BMW Group with its BMW, Mini, and Rolls-Royce brands. The native of Swabia has been in the automotive industry for over 30 years. He is considered not just by people in his industry to be a pioneer of digital transformation. The trained mechanical engineer was elected "CIO of the Year 2018" by the trade press – and even retroactively "CIO of the decade" for the years 2001 to 2011. I've been looking forward to meeting him and talking to him for days. Of course I meet the top IT officer of BMW in Munich, at the IT Center (ITZ) of the corporation, which was completely rebuilt to enable work according to agile principles.

When everyone is involved, there are no losers

The entire building where Klaus Straub works radiates a spirit of change. All over the walls of the BMW IT Center, I read messages related to mind shift. For example, what agility means to the company and what does not. My colleague Sonja Weber from FocusFirst and I meet Klaus Straub in a more or less typical meeting room. However, as in the entire house, there are none of the usual tables arranged in U-shapes and the typical conference chairs. Klaus Straub doesn't like that style at all, as we learn later. He generally prefers bar tables. And he loves the chic café bars scattered throughout the building. They don't just invite you to have a cup of superb coffee but also to hold informal discussions. On this summer day it's so hot that we all drink iced coffee. With lots of ice cubes.

The larger organizations are, the more they need a strategy, a target image. On this point I immediately agree with Klaus Straub. Once an executive knows what direction he or she wants to take, it's his or her job within a corporate to get others involved and to motivate them. I'm interested in how the CIO of BMW realizes that.

"If you take over a team and don't restructure it completely, it's important to actually get every one of them involved," Klaus Straub says. "The classic situation is that there are those who will say, 'Wow, finally we're taking the right direction!' They are intrinsically motivated and immediately present. Then there are those who will find the target image good but don't believe that you can get there. And finally, there's the rest for whom the last 20 years have shown that everything's already done the right way. Now it should be turned into a high-performance team that is intrinsically motivated. That's an enormous issue! Top-down announcements no longer work today. It's better to take a look at sports. Not the top athletic teams but the sports clubs. What motivates people to be tormented by a coach after a day's work? People do it willingly and even pay for it. So there has to be intrinsic motivation. Now you can transfer this to a company and ask yourself: What methodology do I need to get people intrinsically motivated?"

If a sports club is a good role model for Klaus Straub, what does that mean in concrete terms? "First of all, the basic skills have to be there. If an association wants, say, to produce better athletes, the conditions must be right. The same applies to a company: What are the basic skills to achieve maximum performance in the field of IT? That's where you will need to get rid of the fat; the administration has to become leaner; productivity needs to go up, and so on. At BMW, we saw that the digital players – Microsoft, Salesforce, Spotify, Google, Facebook, whatever they're called – have long since established agile software development. We still have a waterfall. Around 2015 there was this massive discussion about the bimodal world and whether a company should have two strings to its bow. If you do that, you'll end up with people who still work according to old principles – kind of like in a bad bank – and you won't get them motivated anymore. Back then we decided in a single lunch workshop: It'll only work if we're 100% agile! Bimodal is not an option. Either everybody will work flexibly – or nobody. Otherwise I will generate winners and losers. I have to get the whole team involved as winners. The board got involved, and then, at the end of 2016, we established a 100 per cent agile IT strategy."

Klaus Straub goes on to explain what the human aspect looked like: "We immediately considered what we wanted to change in our employees' hearts," the CIO states. "So we created, 'We want to have fun!' To understand what that was, you have to realize that IT has long been considered unimportant in the auto industry. IT was everywhere but it wasn't important. People were convinced: 'We can just buy everything from IBM or Accenture.' So IT people never thought about fun but rather about their justification. Now we suddenly said, 'Hey, we're important!' And: 'We want to have fun!' That's how the statement #enjoyIT was born. With a hashtag! I told my 4000 employees at the annual IT Forum: 'Your skills will still be needed even in 20 years from now. We don't know that about many other jobs. But your job is safe.' Savour that. Also to be able to say, 'I'm proud to be an IT specialist.' That was a disruption in the cultural understanding of a car manufacturer. Ten years ago I wouldn't even have dared to say, 'Enjoy IT'. Today our work is accompanied by fun."

That sounds great! So what changed first because of this new mission #enjoyIT? "The whole conversion here. The environment we are sitting in. We completely rebuilt our ITZ. Nobody gave us any money for that." Klaus Straub and his team had no budget for the conversion? And they did it anyway? "We saved the money ourselves, elsewhere, and then built this campus style here. Five years ago there were still nerds running around here who didn't even say hello if you passed them in the hallway. We couldn't believe it. Now we have a very positive atmosphere here, just alone because of the bars with all the trimmings. What was important in our next step: Not only the employees should change, but we on the management level change as well. Today, division managers and senior heads of department all sit in an open space, along with their assistants. My senior head of department and I have foregone huge desks and an office at least three window lengths wide and things like that. We're past that. And that was a significant signal for the employees. They all noticed: Hey, they're serious about it! That was amazing. I didn't expect that. The decentralization of responsibilities came next. Meanwhile teams are given a framework in which they decide for themselves what they do first, what comes second and third. That used to be totally different in the past. 80 to 90 per cent of IT specialists and engineers are happy that they're finally able to make their own decisions. The rest of the people don't really want that. We have to help them."

I detect a lot of appreciation for others in what Klaus Straub is saying. "Appreciation, that's right," he agrees with me. "And at eye level. We're all the same. Of course our responsibility is greater. And sometimes we have to make some tough decisions, too. We also had colleagues who said that we had the wrong IT people and would have to fire 60 per cent of them and get young people from universities. We definitely did not do that. And I think it would've been the wrong way. You have to lead the existing team into the change. What has enormously increased motivation is a programme we call *Back to Code*. We let people who studied software engineering do that themselves again. And not only control 3 000 external specialists, as was customary for a long time with DAX companies. The staff also pushed us to let them do what they had learned. We even have our own academy now. Tomorrow, the first students will graduate and get their certificates. We also don't have many old-fashioned panels anymore. They used to be awful! Today the last panel meets for one hour per month and only to make the decisions that are relevant to compliance. The rest is decided by small groups in World Café mode. That's the next cultural shift: Not everyone is around everywhere where decisions are made. We trust that our colleagues will do a good job. Now you may say: All these ideas were already discussed 5, 10 or 15 years ago. That's true. Our achievement is to implement them! We all have kept our promises. We have got the whole team involved. And we have remained authentic and have never promised more than we could keep."

I want to conclude our conversation by finding out what this authenticity means to Klaus Straub personally. "You have to authentically stand behind all these topics," the BMW CIO explains. "And in my opinion you have to be emotional! It has to be an affair of the heart to promote issues with the executives and the employees. The team will notice whether this is true or not. If I only play a role and stand up in front of them to pull off a show while I already know that I'll be doing something different tomorrow, then I won't get anyone motivated to join me on the road to change."

Getting freelancers involved under the conditions of the "gig economy"

Assuming the responsibility for a well-developed team in a corporation such as the BMW Group and taking just about everyone along on the road to change is a major challenge. This was impressively described by Klaus Straub in our conversation. By contrast, if your team is made up largely or even almost exclusively of freelancers, then your task will be easier and more difficult at the same time. It will be easier because you can usually select external workers as opposed to existing employees, and because you don't have to worry as much about how to handle the 10 or 15 per cent of people who don't fancy epic stuff. At the same time your task will be more difficult because freelancers often have a great emotional distance from the company. Therefore you may not always know what to do to get them involved and motivated. There is also always the danger that freelancers are already looking forward to their next project and therefore stop making your project their top priority – and be it only for economic pressures that many freelancers are subject to.

One thing is certain: In the next few years, dealing with freelancers will become an increasingly important issue. In many areas, we're on our way to becoming a "gig economy", in which people come together for individual projects and then disperse again. Just like musicians who meet, rehearse together, play one or more gigs together and then move on to collaborate with other artists. In music that's been the rule for a long time. What's new is that almost all sectors and professions are moving in that direction. According to future-proofing conducted on behalf of FocusFirst in 2018, more than 40 per cent of the working population in the U.S. will al-

> In many areas, we're on our way to becoming a "gig economy".

ready be in "alternative work arrangements" in five years' time. That will be an increase of 36 per cent within the same period! Five years after that, more than one in two working people might be freelancers. In Western Europe, the pace of that development is slower. But here, too, the trend is unmistakable.

In IT, working with freelancers has long been established. Here you can study what will happen to other industries and areas. Technological development is a key driving force of the gig economy. Today freelancers work for Starbucks or Coffee Fellows and have access to software on their mobile devices that is as efficient as only DAX companies could afford 10 or 15 years ago. Just think of the storage capacity of cloud services, of effective and sometimes even free basic versions of project management solutions – for example, according to the principle of Kanban cards – or of web conferencing tools that can do more than extremely expensive corporate solutions were capable of ten years ago. Freelancers can use these new technologies to control virtual teams of 1 000 or 2 000 people from their bar stools in a coffee bar. The gig economy brings global teams from different nations, cultures and generations, who have diverse life experiences, gender roles and social skills, together. They have different levels of expertise in different fields of knowledge. And all these different people may then become a motivated team that works on a common goal!

Today no leader needs a core team anymore that reports to him or her to do epic stuff. However, working with more and more freelancers increasingly often requires a mind shift in large companies. Basically everything you've read about emotions and intrinsic motivation in this chapter also applies to teams of freelancers – except that all of it becomes even more important! If you no longer have any disciplinary control over employees, all that remains for you to do is to communicate authen-

> Today no leader needs a core team anymore that reports to him or her to do epic stuff.

tically, to arouse their positive emotions and to awaken and maintain their intrinsic motivation. You can hardly lure freelancers with money; at least the best of them can select their clients. There is always money somewhere else. Therefore purpose and showing appreciation become the key factors in the gig economy. Freelancers will jump on a train if they're enthusiastic about the goal and feel acknowledged and appreciated as human beings.

Some people believe that in virtual teams the personal level is not that important because everything becomes "virtual". The opposite is true! The more diverse and global the team is, and the more collaborative the digital channels are, the more important it is to create a sense of togetherness throughout the course of the project and to show appreciation to each and every team member. For major projects, it's a must to get to know each other personally at a kick-off workshop – even if you have to fly to the other end of the world for it. The trust that this will create will more than pay off in the cooperation. Some managers have a problem with highly qualified freelancers because they fear the freelancers might be smarter than they are. In the gig economy, you're glad to see someone join your team who can do more than you in a particular area. It's your job to bring the top of the crop into your team. With this top team you can then ensure that everyone is motivated. That's an art in itself. You will find out in the next chapter what really motivates people.

Chapter 6

The Future in 4D: What Really Motivates People

It was ten to ten on a Wednesday morning. Amelia drove her red Mini quickly through the trendy quarter at the harbor of Dusseldorf. She drove past sparkling glass cubes and refurbished brick warehouses. "You will reach your goal in three hundred metres," the synthetic voice of her navigation system blares. "Your destination is on the right." Amelia's stimulating conversation with her colleague Florian in the passenger seat had ended. The two IT professionals of a consumer goods company apparently thought the same thing: Why are we here? The email from her new project manager, Alain, reads succinctly:

> Our next meeting will be on 23 April at 10:00 a.m. in the rooftop bar "Skyline" at the harbor of Dusseldorf, Speicherstrasse 7. Please be there in time. The reception team on the ground floor has been informed and will be happy to show you the way to the right elevator. We will meet outside on the roof terrace.

Amelia skilfully steered her car into a parking space in front of the glass tower No. 7. She turned off the engine and pulled the handbrake. Florian got out, shut the passenger door and peered at the top of the building. "What're we doing at 10 in the morning in a rooftop bar?" he wondered. Amelia, who had also got out, locked her car with the remote control. "Well, we'll find out in five minutes," she retorted glibly.

When Amelia and Florian had crossed the deserted bar on the 20th floor and stepped out onto the roof terrace, their colleagues were already there. They stood at bar tables, having coffee, tea or sparkling water. A waiter asked Amelia and Florian what they wanted to drink; both ordered cappuccino. It was sunny but chilly, so everybody kept their jackets and coats on. Everyone, except for Project Manager Alain, who was leaning against the balustrade of the terrace, dressed in jeans, a white shirt and a dark blue blazer. Behind him, the Rhine tower rose up and they could see the old town. It was a stunning panorama! Alain nodded to Amelia and Florian and then looked around contentedly. They were complete now. Alain took two steps forward and straightened his back.

"Good morning, folks," Alain started, "and welcome to a little journey into the future. We will now watch a film together. This film will be entirely in your minds, so Amelia will see a slightly different film than Florian or Robert. But that's okay. Are you ready?" He registered perplexity but not irritation in the team members' faces. The project manager apparently knew exactly what he was doing here – everyone in the team could sense that. "It's the 23rd of July," Alain continued, "exactly three months from now. I'm standing here and you're standing where you're right now. But it's not ten a. m. but ten p. m. It's a warm summer evening. The sun has set and it's dusky. We can see beautiful colours, ranging from dark blue to yellow to red. The Rhine tower is lit and its lights are flashing. Behind it you can see the old town and the evening skyline of the city centre. It's like on a city poster, only that it's real. Can you see it?"

Some team members had closed their eyes; others were paying close attention to Alain's words. Everybody was silent. Nobody moved. Alain continued, "There's a soft and pleasant breeze that circulates the warm air. The bar area is filled with loungy jazz sounds played by our band. You're having cocktails mixed by the city's hottest bartender, whom we've hired for tonight. There are flowers everywhere; their scent is wonderful. Right there in the centre there is a five-layer champagne cake. Before we cut the cake, we congratulate each other. We congratulate everyone for completing this project within three months. We congratulate each other because it has turned out fantastic, and our internal customers and users are super happy with the new solution. When it's dark, a laser light show starts. First the name of our project appears in the evening sky, then each one of your names: Susanne, Mark, Kevin, Robert, Amelia, Florian, … There is applause for every name."

"I have goosebumps," Florian whispered to Amelia. "Me too," she replied. "It's going to be an absolutely beautiful evening. And it will be in just three months!" Florian raised his eyebrows. "We still have a lot of work to do till then." Amelia smiled at her colleague and said, "So what? It'll be a breeze."

Excellence due to the right mental technique

Whenever top performance is achieved today – be it in top-level athletics, in emergency medicine, by anti-terrorist police units, or in space travel – mental coaching is used. One of the most important instruments of mental coaching is so-called visualization. In this technique, a single coachee or team guided by a coach experiences a future situation in their minds. And they experience it as intensely as if it were real. It's like running a film in your head that shows the future in all its facets. The goal is mentally anticipated. After that, it's as if the brain had already experienced that situation. And our brain classifies everything we've ever experienced as something that is repeatable. If the goal seemed to have been – almost – unattainable prior to the visu-

> One of the most important instruments of mental coaching is so-called visualization.

alization, it will seem feasible after applying this mental technique. But that's not all: If it was part of the visualization to anticipate the happy sensation that sets in after having achieved the goal, your subconscious is now programmed to actually experience these sensations. Then you are highly motivated to do everything in order to experience that state of happiness that already felt so wonderful in your mind. How great must it be to experience it in real life!

The term "visualization" – derived from Latin "viso" = "I see" – is actually too narrow a term, for in mental coaching you don't use the visual sense channel for a long time in order to mentally anticipate future events. Today, mental coaches work with 4-D or even 5-D scenarios, in which the auditory, the olfactory, the haptic and possibly even the gustatory senses are addressed. In mental coaching, the future event should be seen, heard, felt, smelled, and – in some cases – even tasted (in the form of the champagne cake that will be served at the celebration party for Alain's project team, for example.) You may have experienced it in one of these cinemas where the seats wobble, water splashes on the audience or fragrance cartridges provide certain smells: The audience dives into the film with (almost) all of their senses. Actually, one should rather speak of "simulation" than of "visualization". I use both terms synonymously in this chapter. That is, when I use the term "visualization", I usually mean mental techniques that address multiple sensory channels simultaneously.

> For decades, the U.S. space centre NASA has been working successfully with mental coaching for its astronauts.

Take aerospace as an example of how visualizations or simulations are used: For decades, NASA has been working successfully with mental coaching for its astronauts. The special thing about space travel is that life in space can only be practiced inadequately on Planet Earth by someone who has never been out there before.

With a so-called parabolic flight on which a normal passenger plane briefly goes into free fall, weightlessness can be generated for only 20 seconds. The budding astronauts will spend days, weeks or even months in weightlessness. Even breathing in weightlessness can be practiced with certain techniques. The same applies to food consumed directly from bags and tubes, fitness training without gravity or going to the bathroom, which turns into a challenging feat. But training everything at once? Only mental coaching can do that. NASA has its astronauts go through every detail of the situation in space over and over again before it finally saying, "We have a lift-off." Space travel is extremely expensive. Therefore NASA wants to make absolutely sure that their astronauts are up to the situation and will never feel overwhelmed by it. The simulations in training provide for that.

Mental coaching is most common in competitive sports. Almost all top athletes today have mental coaches: swimmers, runners, high jumpers, shot-putters, weight lifters, and so on. Yet mental coaching is also used in team sports. Many clubs in the German Bundesliga, the English Premier League, or the American football and basketball leagues NFL and NBA, have a permanent mental coach on their payrolls. These are usually sports psychologists with a university degree. Here, mental simulations are part of everyday life. A basketball player repeatedly visualizes in slow motion how he jumps up, holding the ball, what he sees on his left and his right, and how he then pushes the ball into the basket with his fingertips pointing slightly down. Every tiny detail of such a "dunk" is anticipated and acted out. Not just once, but over and over again. That's exactly what soccer players do when practicing penalty kicks, free kicks, traps, and so on. In mental coaching, extreme climbers memorize almost every square inch of the wall they will climb without a safety rope. They feel with their fingertips the exact rock formation in each particular spot and know exactly where to put their hands and feet next.

What athletes keep visualizing and simulating again and again is the moment of success: that buzzing feeling after climbing the summit. Bathing in endorphins when the swimmer takes off her goggles and can tell by looking at the clock that she has beaten the world record. The marathon runner's indescribable feeling of relief and joy the moment he crosses the finish line with both his feet. Such simulations of perfect happiness have a powerful pull effect and let us – consciously, but even more subconsciously – do everything we can to really experience such happiness. This element of the simulation can therefore be transferred particularly well to other areas of life. To significant personal wishes: for instance, how to find the right partner. And specially to major business goals. The good fortune of a successful business start-up can be anticipated mentally as well as the achievement of a challenging project goal. The 4-D movie in your head can show you how soon you will be a head of department, a division manager or even board member. You can also visualize how you and your team make the first million, the first ten million or even the first hundred million euros ever made in annual sales – and how you will celebrate it!

> Such simulations of perfect happiness have a powerful pull effect and let us – consciously, but even more subconsciously – do everything we can to really experience such happiness.

When I founded FocusFirst, I visualized from the start the success that I desired for my company, my family and myself ten years later. I built that simulation in my mind for weeks, adding more and more details. From time to time, I still sit down in a quiet place and let this film run through my head. FocusFirst has long since made a huge leap towards that film. Yet the simulation still feels gigantic. It has a wow effect. Some details of my simulation are very personal. But I'd like to share the most important scenarios with you to stimulate your own mental films and your imagination. Later in this chapter, I'll give you specific tips on what to look for when developing simulations for yourself or your team.

It's 7 p. m. on 1 July 2025, and I'm in Singapore. I'm sitting in a smart sports car (I'll let you guess the brand …) with my wife and our two daughters, and we're heading for an ultra-modern skyscraper. The building has a glass facade and is built close to the water. I visualize how the steering wheel feels; I run my finger over the seams and smell the leather. Swing music is playing on the entertainment system. I see my daughters in the rear-view mirror and imagine what they're talking about. We park in a reserved parking space in front of the skyscraper, get out of the car and link arms. We are dressed festively. I also visualize all details of our clothes. We enter the building – the sliding door opens with a soft hissing sound – and arrive in a light-flooded, pleasantly cool atrium. Hundreds of people are waiting for us under a banner that reads "FocusFirst 2025 – Goal Achieved": employees, clients, business partners, family members, friends, former colleagues. Confetti is raining from the ceiling. To the right of the entrance, a big band is playing, and a deceptively genuine Sinatra impersonator sings "New York, New York" from the top of his lungs. (Okay, we're in Singapore, but that doesn't matter because I love that song!)

Now I visualize many more details of the party: I know whom I'm hugging and whom I'm giving a high five. I taste the champagne after we have clinked glasses. As soon as the party is at its peak, I take one of the glass elevators by myself up to the 37th floor. I get off the elevator and step into my office, which is on that floor in 2025. The glass walls provide a fantastic view. On the right there is my desk made of olive wood, my old, saddle-brown Chesterfield desk chair behind it. I notice one or two sheets of paper on the desktop, as well as my MacBook and a plain white vase filled with fresh tulips. I walk over to the floor-to-ceiling window front, touch the somewhat cold pane with my fingers, look over the harbor, the islands and hundreds of tankers that seem to be barely moving. So much movement yet so much serenity! As I let my gaze wander around the room, my wife and two daughters come up to me from behind. They wrap their arms around me from my right and my left – no one says anything. Silence. We just smile and are incredibly grateful for what we have achieved so far and can now experience.

So this is the simulation I developed during the founding phase of FocusFirst. How did you feel while reading it? Maybe you thought: Absolutely fantastic! Or you might have thought: Well, not bad. Either is okay because it's my personal simulation. And that's not what this chapter is really about. The point is that *you*, as the head of epic stuff, will be able to develop your own simulation for yourself and your team. For your own big goals and those of your team and yourself. Your vision might look completely different than the scenario in Singapore in 2025 you've just mentally witnessed. But what may be similar are these three elements: Your simulation is great and impressive and contains nothing that's already daily stuff for you anyway or that will be easily accessible in a few weeks or months. Secondly, it activates several sensory channels simultaneously. Thirdly, it contains many, many details that are fun for you or your team and a reflection of your respective values and preferences.

But beware: Mental techniques are not an end in themselves! If you have a spontaneous idea for a simulation now, then ask yourself first to what extent the target image that's behind it is really coherent. Only then should you get ready to work on it. So before I'll tell you what to look for when developing your visualization in detail, I want to introduce you to a leader who, in my opinion, stands for harmonious visions. In his career Christoph Hüls has repeatedly succeeded in adjusting people to big goals with the help of emotional images. He knows both the corporate world and the world of start-ups. Christoph was Head of Innovation Strategy at Merck, then managed a protein analysis start-up and later returned

> **Mental techniques are not an end in themselves!**

to Merck as an internal entrepreneur in action. During our conversation I want to find out how he developed powerful visions of the future in both a young and an established company and planted them in his team members' heads.

A good vision will create a common future

I meet Dr. Christoph Hüls in a small, charming coffee bar in a superbly restored old building in Darmstadt. It's a lovely, warm summer day and the windows are wide open. We sit on beautiful classic chairs made of solid wood at a square table and enjoy excellent coffee. Christoph is an out and out visionary person; at least that's how I have always perceived him. Today I ask him directly, "How do you manage to plant your vision – or if you don't want to call it vision, then perhaps your target image – in people's minds? I mean, you don't just go to a start-up, for instance, and build up the company successfully for seven years. There must be something that makes you and your team stick to it. That makes you all do your best to be successful. You couldn't have done that by yourself. So what did you do to make others follow you and support you?"

"That's absolutely correct, René. As a new manager of the start-up I knew that I couldn't do it on my own, and so I quickly got external help. Most start-ups don't do that, and – just as an anecdote on the side – it gave those who had brought me aboard some serious hiccups at first. But in the end I was able to convince everybody that it was the right thing to do. We were 36 people at the time, and I said, 'Now we have to create a common vision!' Most of them thought it was a waste of time. But then I got the entire company to do a two-day offsite with an external coach and do nothing but work on our vision for the full two days. It was a great feeling to walk through the company and see how our vision was stuck to the screens and then realized. For me as managing director that was almost like a salvation: Finally everyone had a common goal and was running in the same direction! It's true that even in a company with only 36 people there are silos – personal preferences and preferred ways of doing things that are not always the best for the company. That's where the shared vision comes into play. And the key to it may be that you, as their leader, demonstrate it first, with every fibre of your body. *That's* leadership. Period."

I want to know how Christoph later transferred this visionary approach to a corporate. After all, he was first in a corporate, then in a start-up, and then returned to another large corporate environment. How did he take his expertise with him? After all, the structures are quite different – and defining your own goals leads to much greater conflicts of interest in a corporate. "That's a huge challenge," Christoph replies. "I mean, visions have always existed in larger organizations. They are written down somewhere on paper or in PowerPoint. But, frankly, they're not realized, and frequently not everybody knows about them. So far I've always tried to create our own identity in the troop I had to lead. With the proviso that I need connection points, of course. I've always tried to clarify what our goal is, what we stand for and what our contribution to the big picture is. And then it was always: a clear focus on it! We focus on this goal! I've never set goals with PowerPoint presentations; instead I've always worked them out together with the people. In the end, everyone has to make the goal their own and live it, not just me."

Most of the teams in companies still don't bother to create their own vision away from the corporate vision. What advice does Christoph have for those who want to take that step? What were typical visions he developed together with his teams? What makes a good vision and how do you get there? "For me, the rational component, the clear goal, is where you start," Christoph explains. "The direction I want to take must be clear. Then it's the emotion, the passion, for me. Being a start-up, the shortest formula for our vision was, 'Health is our passion.' Now you may say that's quite exaggerated for a small service company doing protein analytics for pharmaceutical corporations. But that was just the core of the whole thing. The people who created this together all had their own personal stories. Everyone felt passionately about contributing to the improvement of the health of people all over the world."

> Most of the teams in companies still don't bother to create their own vision away from the corporate vision.

The vision was apparently linked to personal stories, emotions, and therefore activated more senses than any phrase, such as "We're the most successful company in our field" would have. Would Christoph say that he created a future together with his team? "That's right," he confirms. "And I always try to do that. I was Head of Technology Foresight & Scouting at a DAX-30 corporation, which focused on developing its innovation strategy. I set up a very young team within a year. And to give you an idea of the image we created: We called ourselves the 'Masters of the Innoverse'. That said a lot about our vision, includ-

> We called ourselves the 'Masters of the Innoverse'.

ing that allusion to 'Masters of the Universe', namely that we create a new world, a new universe, through innovations. We wanted to be the ones who saw something new outside and then promote it inside the corporation. So we had a huge and powerful goal. At the same time, what we did had this pirate-like character: We explicitly let ourselves be different. Break rules. We really wanted to do something different than what a corporate normally does."

Pirates – how exciting! The target image "health is our passion" probably provided everyone with their own image, each image being different. That's not a bad thing – after all, all that matters is that everyone can relate to it. "Masters of the Innoverse" and the "pirates" who deliberately break rules – that's already quite a grand image in comparison to "health is our passion". These are extremely powerful images that create a sense of belonging, adding fun and excitement. Finally I want to know what working on the "pirate ship" was like. "The atmosphere was just incredibly creative and everybody was looking ahead," Christoph recalls. "Productive, innovative and ultimately very successful. Nobody was afraid to speak up or go their own unconventional ways. Everything was addressed bluntly. After all, we were pirates! And as for the sense of belonging, the affiliation: When I quit that job and my team broke up, I was accused of having broken up a family!"

The makings of a really good film about the future

A pharmaceutical and chemical corporation feared destruction on a much larger scale when Frank – yes, his name really *was* Frank – came up with a plan to burn pyrotechnics on the premises of a chemical plant. Did he intend to blow up the whole plant? Not at all! Frank manages a challenging global project in that corporation. It was really difficult. And tedious. To motivate his team, he and FocusFirst started to look for a spectacular idea for a party for everyone to celebrate the successful completion of the project together. It was supposed to be something nobody had ever dreamed of doing before. And then we came up with the idea of having fireworks on the premises of the plant. At first no one could believe that something like that would ever happen. But Frank literally painted a brightly coloured vision of the fireworks. And what can I say? After Frank and his team had successfully completed their project and were overjoyed, everone gathered on the roof of a building that overlooked the gigantic chemical site one evening. There was a DJ, delicious food, superb drinks, a cheerful atmosphere. But actually everybody just talked about topic: What about the fireworks? Finally, when darkness set in, the big moment came: Under the watchful eyes of the plant's firemen, the chemical plant was illuminated by a spectacular pyro show. Some still couldn't believe it: For the first time in the history of the chemical industry, firecrackers were lit for fun at a chemical plant. At the same time it was probably the craziest party in a positive way that has ever been thrown at this time-honoured corporation.

No matter what your ideas for visions and emotions, for target images and motivating incentives ultimately look like: Create a wow effect! On your own or with your team, think of things that are not run-of-the-mill. Being a pirate in a corporate is not run-of-the-mill. And illuminating a chemical site with pyrotechnics is definitely not, either. Ultimately it will always depend on the team what's perceived as being commonplace and what's spectacular. In some companies, there is still so little

> Create a wow effect! On your own or with your team, think of things that are not run-of-the-mill.

emotion and so little connectedness that the prospect of a rooftop bar party is absolutely extraordinary. In contrast, you probably won't be able to thrill a team of global consultants, who always attend after-work parties in the rooftop bars of Hong Kong, Rio de Janeiro or L. A., with the prospect of throwing a party on the rooftops of Dusseldorf. For that reason I mainly describe the mental technique in this chapter. You will find exemplary images and events. Ultimately you must discover for yourself what suits you and your team.

I fully agree with Christoph Hüls that it makes sense to start with the rational side. Before you develop a simulation that will implant a desired future into the heads of your team, check your goal. Is it realistic and consistent? Big, but not too big? That's exactly the challenge – as I've stated earlier in this book. Again, take sports as an example. If an athlete wanted to run 100 metres at the speed of light, it wouldn't be a realistic goal. This is science fiction and simply absurd. Even if his goal was to make it in five seconds, I'm still skeptical if that would really motivate him. It's just too far out of reach. But if you have a very challenging but generally achievable goal, then you can begin to envision the future for yourself and your team. What will it feel like in the end? How will you perceive your goal with your four senses? If the state of having reached your goal is rather abstract and not very tangible – for example, a specific sales target, which is ultimately just a number – then ask yourself: How will you celebrate the achievement of the goal? And how exactly will that be – down to the details?

Before I give you a step-by-step guide to a successful visualization at the end of this chapter, I'd like to share some practical tips with you while warning you about a few pitfalls. First of all, it's important that your team members can really see these visions and images. The film is in their heads – and only there. Please don't give in to the temptation to actually make a film. If I had my Singapore simulation staged by a film crew with actors and then watched it on my tablet while drinking a glass of wine at night, the effect would have been almost zero. No matter how many times I would have rerun the film. Simulations only work if we really let them develop in our minds. This is the only way we can anticipate the future. When we watch a film, we don't watch it from the protagonist's perspective either. We look at an event from the outside. That contradicts the principle of mental engineering.

I have already commented on the wow effect. This is its scientific background: Our brain focuses its attention on what is new, different or important. So when creating visualizations, make sure that these elements occur if possible: something new, something unexpected, and something that's important to people. No one had ever seen pyrotechnics on the site of the chemical plant before Frank's par-

> **Our brain focuses its attention on what is new, different or important.**

ty, for instance. That was a totally novel experience. It was also radically different from what one would expect from a chemical plant where operational safety is paramount. (In fact, the fireworks were not dangerous at all; they only sounded dangerous to people who don't know anything about pyrotechnics – and that was exactly what made the wow effect happen.) And finally, the controlling of one's attention based on importance – something everybody is probably familiar with: You think of purchasing a specific car model – and suddenly you see that car model everywhere you go. When that car model wasn't yet important to you, you didn't notice how many of these cars were around. So think about what's important to you and your team. That will guarantee that you pay attention to it.

The future in 4D, visualization or simulation, is the fuel on your way to big goals. However, make sure you don't burn too much fuel. When you overstretch a visualization, it will lose its power. For example, I have always shared my Singapore visualization only in special situations: at kick-off events or when people have just joined our team. Talking about it in every meeting would be counterproductive. Now and then it can be helpful to work with smaller, complementary simulations. But keep in mind that this is a mental technique for ambitious goals and should not be used for things that are likely to occur anyway. For example, if you don't have a budget for a project, but it's just a question of negotiating skills and patience until the money becomes available, you don't need to visualize anything. If the budget issue is critical and could fail, it may of course be part of your film, as well as that the money is granted and everyone is happy.

When I write in detail about a mental technique in this chapter, I don't want to conceal the fact that there are people who will doubt its effect. Sometimes I hear statements such as, "I know that, I tried it, it doesn't work!" Apart from the fact that space agencies or special police or military units know what they're doing when they rely on mental training: In a case like that, I ask first of all how much time that individual has taken for the development of visualizations or simulations? Did the person really sit down in a quiet spot? Did he or she envision the details? Did they activate several sensory channels? Did they repeat the whole scenario frequently, adding new details? Usually they didn't.

Sometimes I hear a very different objection: "If mental training really worked and all the top athletes used it, then all would ultimately be winners." Obviously they are not. A marathon runner may have visualized her goal a hundred times and still suffer from muscle cramps and give up after 32 kilometres on the day of the race. Why is that? Because life is life. It's highly complex. And success can never be 100 per cent planned in advance. Athletes may have a bad day; missile launches are postponed due to bad weather; special forces missions fail. That's how it is. Mental techniques significantly increase the probability of success. No more and no less. The fact that people can always fail doesn't mean that mental training doesn't work. Another example to illustrate that fact: Seat belts and airbags significantly increase the chance of survival in a serious car accident. Nevertheless, people die in their cars. To conclude from that that seat belts and airbags are useless would be illogical. Even though there can be no guaranteed success, the future presented in 4D is what really motivates people.

> Mental techniques significantly increase the probability of success. No more and no less.

Creating completely new processes due to the right vision

I'm going to Bonn and am looking forward to talking to another leader who is driven by powerful visions: Nils Stamm, the first Chief Digital Officer of Telekom Germany, started in the former state-owned company as a "one-man show", he says – with the challenging task of putting the Number One on track in the German market regarding digital transformation. The Bavarian, who is in his mid-forties, is not only a jock – including a CrossFit fan, a surfer and snowboarder – but also enjoyed a fast-paced career before he was offered his current position: As a young business administrator, Nils started to work for a hip agency before he went to Web.de at the peak of the New Economy. There he immediately took care of the monetization of the entire search machine business. (Those were the days when Google was still just one search engine among many.) Later, he was responsible for telephonic value-added services in various countries from London. He built up virtually the whole e-commerce system, including its online store, for O2 in Munich. Via additional stations at United Internet – today the parent company of his first employer, Web. de – the motorcycle fan finally came to Telekom. We meet at the company headquarters next to the former "diplomats' racetrack", Freeway 7 between the centre of Bonn and Bad Godesberg. The ultra-modern building also houses a Telekom shop on the ground floor that presents the latest products of the corporation. This is where we'll take a selfie after our talk.

The Telekom expected from their new CDO to jump right into major projects from the start. That makes Nils an ideal conversation partner for me on the topic of visions and goals in large organizations. How do you achieve good goals in corporates?

"For me, it's fundamental to bring a vision across," Nils explains. "Here at Telekom Deutschland I had complete freedom and the opportunity to first define what digital transformation would mean to us. So first I developed my vision and then, in a second step, I translated it into concrete business goals that would give the whole thing its purpose and make the vision tangible. The third step was to break it all down: What exactly do I have to accomplish to achieve the goals – both organizationally and in the sense of rather concrete, individual changes? I could never do that by myself but rather have to meet the others halfway. While doing so, I take a psychological approach. Though hierarchy is required – you need a certain position from which you can initiate changes – that won't get people to stand behind you. For it you need visions and communication."

I want to know what vision that was. "The best digital customer experience," Nils says, adding, "We'll create the best digital experience for our customers on our digital touchpoints, i. e. on all websites, in all apps, and whenever customers interact digitally with us. We're not there yet, but we're definitely on our way; we're getting faster and faster in the things we do, and they keep getting easier, too." I also find this vision as such easy – in the sense of extremely easy to understand. I'm interested in how Nils and his team proceeded to translate that, how they conveyed the vision in day-to-day operations. "I have to be able to imagine the status when a goal has been achieved," Nils explains. "Of course, it helps to look at other companies that have already managed to achieve what we want to do. To have tangible examples. That's the second thing. The third is to not only communicate to your own people how the customers will benefit from the vision but also how it will make things easier and better for them: 'What's in it for me?' That purpose must be conveyed."

> While doing so, I take a psychological approach. Though hierarchy is required – you need a certain position from which you can initiate changes – that won't get people to stand behind you. For it you need visions and communication.

So how did Nils go about it? He sums it up into three major issues: "Agile transformation, IT transformation, and finally, really implementing the digital business." Nils lists details and examples of all three issues: "Transformation towards agile work methods means that all our in-house units that are scattered in different companies are turned into one large superordinate tribe – let me just call it tribe – and collaborate completely cross-functionally and across all barriers. For example, we introduced OKRs, objectives and key results. What this means for everyone, in tangible quarterly terms, is: What would I like to achieve as an individual, with the team and as a superordinate unit, as a value stream? Everyone positions themselves there – yet it's still not a target system! This is very important! We don't check the results but rather say: 70 per cent of your OKRs are already very good! We want everyone to always set themselves somewhat higher goals than they can actually achieve. It's all about learning. And about measurability."

What about IT? "We're completely converting it to the front end. Telko had always been working with large releases before. We've managed to get out of that and to change our front ends, i. e. really the digital customer interface, at each spot daily. Do we do that perfectly already? No. But we do it much, much better than we did two years ago." And the products? The actual digital business with end customers? "Before it had been like this: If we had a new product, it went into the shop, and the salesperson, who was intelligent, could explain it really well. No matter how sophisticated the product was, the seller managed to bring it across to you. A website couldn't do that. Here we have now arranged for a complete mindshift: A product idea is first tested online. How does it work for the customer on the web? If it works there, it will work everywhere in our company. So at the hotline and in the shop, too, for instance. That means we actually turned the model around."

> Here, "change" wasn't "managed"; instead there was an inspired focus.

I think that's a very nice example of how a vision can be transformed in the end. Here, "change" wasn't "managed"; instead there was an inspired focus and a simple, clear and powerful vision which, broken down into day-to-day operations, led to new and much more effective approaches. I want to know next if Nils had also experienced any particularly emotional moments as CDO of Telekom Germany.

"Yes, in two ways – negative as well as positive," he explains. "Negative, because our first transformation model was not successful and we therefore hit rock bottom. First of all, we had to admit to ourselves that: Hey, that great big engine we started isn't working; we have to make some fundamental changes. A corporation like Telekom is not used to changing major things just like that. But we had the courage to do it. It was great that the board agreed immediately: Yes, that's right, we have to do it differently. That was a great vote of trust, which triggered very strong positive emotions in me. That much trust really motivated me even more and created the emotional basis for everything else. Another extremely powerful moment, not only for me, but for my entire team, was when we could work with the management to establish a completely new decision-making process for digital and agile issues. Now we call it the QBR, the quarterly business review, and it's based on the fact that, like Amazon, we only submit two pages of text with our main points. Then we spend 30 minutes talking about impediments alone, i. e. things we need from management to solve problems. No more lengthy presentations, no big discussions in the panel procedure, nothing. The feedback was overwhelmingly positive. Everyone came and said that they always wanted to do it this way from now on, in other areas as well. That was an extremely powerful moment."

I can imagine it vividly. Finally, I want to know from Nils where he would still like to go. "The sky's the limit", he answers spontaneously, laughing. "That's how things are with us. But what we really want is a high level of automation. For what we're doing today requires a lot of workforce. And when I look at the big picture, I say: Right now we're very much concerned with the question how we do things and how we can make them better. How we can realize an agile work method, for instance. At the next stage of evolution, we will no longer deal with the *how* but only with the *what*. When we're at that point, my job will be done, so to speak. Then the transformation will be complete."

Step by step to a simulation that will really motivate people

My ambition is to give you insights into how visions in large companies become reality and what will really motivate you and your people to work towards big goals through all the ups and downs along the way. I have introduced you to the mental technique of visualization or simulation, described why it works so well and showed you how to use it for your goals. In addition, you've learned from inspiring leaders how to develop visions, get people to come aboard and, finally, to make sure their visions become daily business reality step by step. In this last section, I would like to tie all threads together again. The whole thing is a bit of a left-brain-right-brain theme: There's the rational and the emotional side.

First of all, you define a vision and corresponding goals that are strategic, achievable, clear, and comprehensible. Then you add emotion to the whole thing. You invent a story, make a mental film. Now, if

> A really good simulation releases as many endorphins as if the goal had already been reached.

you were to ask me which aspect is the more important one, I would say: the emotional one. The rational side is more of a foundation. A coherent foundation is important. But if you don't touch your team emotionally, it will be useless. You need the endorphins! And a really good simulation releases as many endorphins as if the goal had already been reached.

Here is a systematic guide for your visualization or simulation as a turbo on your way to the big goal:

1. In the first step you define the exact goal and make yourself aware of it. Limit yourself to a single goal: *one goal.* In Chapter 3, I described how to get to that one big goal by setting the right priorities. Now make that goal concrete. In this first step, numbers, dates and facts are beneficial, for example: "On December 31st, 2024, we achieved an annual turnover of more than 100 million euros with our new product." Perhaps it doesn't pertain to sales but instead, for instance, to successfully introducing some specific software by a certain date. Then define the exact criteria for success. What has to be fulfilled so that the project can be completed successfully? Or – another example – it's about the vision to be completely digital in a particular area by Day X. In that case, also define the criteria for achieving the goal as accurately as possible.

2. In your next step, develop a story about the vision. For instance, what's the perfect moment after you've achieved the goal? What is that state like, and what do and your team experience? Example: A sales or growth target for the next five or ten years is very abstract. Therefore ask yourself what exactly will change in your daily work life when that goal has been reached? Will you and your team be sitting in a brand new building because you're creating so much value now that you can afford it? Will everybody drive even classier company cars and fly business instead of economy? Will there be free meals, such as Google & other corporations provide? Or might there rather be changes in immaterial things? Has the foundation for tending to the purpose of your work with much more serenity, time and leisure been laid? Will there be more time for social commitments now? Or will you be able to just take time off more often? The story should definitely contain elements of something new, different or important. It needs a certain wow effect. A spectacular party to celebrate your success is always an option.

3. Now collect plenty of material to make your story concrete. Ensure that the images you want to create are tangible and realistic. In the introductory story of this chapter, project leader Alain checked out the location – and later showed it to his team – where he wants to celebrate the completion of the project with an unforgettable evening. And, of course, in Singapore I stood in front of the windows of one of the top floors of a glass highrise and looked at the water and the harbour. I can mentally recall that view at any given time. Or, suppose you want to have created a new work environment in the end. Then you might want to go to furniture and designer shops and even touch what they are selling. Spend time on details so you can also visualize these details!

4. In your next step, you assemble the actual film chronologically in your head. Start with a key visual, such as "rooftop bar", "fireworks", "new office", and so on. Then invent – like a screenwriter and director all rolled into one – a longer sequence and go through it step by step. Always stay positive, concrete, in the first-person perspective and in the present. But not like: "There will be employees standing around and toasting each other." Rather: "I turn around and see Amelia and Florian toasting each other with a glass of champagne, smiling." Staying positive means that you only visualize what is happening and not what's not happening. So don't imagine: "I'm not sweating." Instead: "The temperature is pleasant and I feel good."

5. Now play the film over and over again in your mind just for yourself. Do this in a silent and safe place. It's therefore advisable that you don't have to run off to get to an appointment soon or are waiting at the overcrowded gate of an airport to take a plane. Make sure you are able to relax. In a relaxed state, it is easiest to be imaginative and creative. By running your film over and over again, you'll keep coming up with new details. Integrate the most wonderful details

into your film. You may find that your film will touch you more emotionally with each time you watch it. Make sure that the film really does stay only in your head. Don't make any videos, not even to complement the vision!

6. When your mental film is completed, tell others about it. First describe it only to your close confidants and then to a larger group. Describe the film the way you see it in your head and always from the first-person perspective. For example: "I step out of the elevator on the top floor, meet Amelia and Florian and give them both a warm hug. Then we walk out to the terrace together. The band is playing *Take Five*." You can also tell the film to a larger group in a suitable setting. Make sure no one is under time pressure and everyone can listen to you attentively. An all-day offsite for the start of a project makes for a suitable framework, for instance. Also describe your film to every new member of your team. Keep telling everything again and again but don't overdo it. Rely on your sense of the right moment for the film.

I have already described my Singapore film for FocusFirst very often – and still describe it periodically. Sometimes even I still get goosebumps while telling it. This is a clear indication of how much a simulation triggers in your body. And do you know what's funny? By now no one wonders anymore if FocusFirst will actually be able to achieve its big goal by 1 July 2025. Instead, people are wondering what they will wear to the party or at which airport and with which airline they'll be able to fly in. So a really big future goal will eventually become a natural reality in people's minds. The next chapter focuses on how this reality will actually come true.

Chapter 7

Go Big or Stay Home: Now You Will Deliver

Subway station "Münchner Freiheit", Tuesday evening, shortly after 8 p. m. As always, Susan took the stairs from the underground platform to street level. The top manager who worked in the sales department of a worldwide insurance company only used escalators or elevators in absolutely exceptional cases. For instance, when she was traveling to art exhibitions on weekends with her elderly mother. Or when she had older male colleagues in tow who, after decades in the insurance company, had become not only a bit unimaginative but also lethargic. Fortunately, there were only a few of those in her own working area. When Susan started her job as a newcomer to the industry about six months ago, she had found a young team that was easily motivated. Only the unsuccessful years working for her predecessor still dampened the team's spirits a bit. The team members simply missed a sense of achievement.

Susan had been the company's white hope. From Day One, however, she had done everything in her power to let her team forget that fact. She introduced herself warmly and openly, addressed everyone by their first names – a practice that wasn't generally common yet in the conservative culture of the German corporation – and made no one feel that she was the boss. As an outsider of the insurance industry, she initially had lots of questions – and absolutely no qualms to ask them. At the same time she announced in the very first meeting with her team: "From now on we will be doing epic things. We'll get the clients we've only been dreaming of. You can look forward to it! It's going to happen." One of the habits that made Susan different from her predecessor was that she took the subway to the office instead of driving to work in a heavy limousine, the size of a company car allotted to anyone at her level. And of course the fact that she always took the stairs instead of the elevator. The manager, who was in her late thirties, just wasn't comfortable with taking the easy way out.

After climbing the stairs up several levels, Susan reached the exit three minutes later. The streets were still hustling and bustling on this warm evening at the beginning of summer. Almost all outdoor seats of the restaurants and cafés were taken. Instead of keeping to the left, in the direction of her old apartment, Susan turned right, walked around the corner and quickly headed towards the Reveka supermarket that was tucked away on a side street. Susan had already stopped by Reveka the evening before, just like every evening of the previous week. Her fridge was crammed with food. But she wasn't the only one with a full refrigerator. Everybody in her team shopped at Reveka's every day – either in the morning before work, at lunchtime or on their way home, just as Susan was doing. And everyone took lots of pictures for their WhatsApp group called "Reveka".

Reveka was one of the largest food store chains in Germany with around 75 billion euros in sales per year. Susan wanted to win Reveka as a client. Her predecessor had tried to do just that in vain for six years. He hadn't shopped even once at Reveka. His housekeeper had done all the food shopping for his family. If Susan's unlucky predecessor had been asked where the nearest Reveka supermarket to his house in Munich's suburb of Grünwald was, he would probably have been as perplexed as if someone had asked him which detergent his shirts had been washed with. Susan had been trying for three months to get the big fish called Reveka on the hook. That included daily contact with the brand – for everyone in her team! Susan had come up with the idea of the WhatsApp group and the photos one morning on her way to the subway.

The Reveka food market in the heart of the Schwabing district was still crowded when Susan went in through the automatic sliding doors. She grabbed a shopping basket, went to the fruit and vegetable department and selected a bunch of organic bananas, a bowl of blueberries and a bag of lamb's lettuce. A young sales clerk was filling a shelf with brightly coloured bell peppers. "Hello, good evening!" Susan said to her. "You're still so active for your customers tonight. I think that's great! I'm Susan and I work for the future insurance partner of the Reveka Group. Would you like to take a quick selfie of us for our in-house WhatsApp group? That would be great!" At first the sales clerk looked a bit surprised, but Susan's smile was infectious. "Sure, why not?" she said.

A few moments later the two women stood in front of the bell pepper shelf, beaming into the camera. Holding the smartphone, Susan stretched her arm and pushed the trigger. After thanking the sales clerk, she uploaded the photo to WhatsApp. Her message: "Schwabing, 8.30 p. m. Everybody working for our next major client is still cheerful and fully motivated☺" After posting the message, Susan scrolled the WhatsApp group site up and looked at the other pictures of the day: a selfie with a cashier; some shopping bags with the Reveka logo on a park bench in the English garden. Also, a portrait of a cute Yorkshire terrier leashed in front of a Reveka store. "Man, that should work tomorrow, I just know it!" Susan thought as she put her phone away. Another video conference with the Reveka headquarters in Cologne was planned for tomorrow.

Do epic stuff – and don't just think about it

So as not to keep you on tenterhooks: After only three months, Susan actually got the key account her predecessor had been unsuccessfully trying to get for six years with the same team. In real life, Susan has a different name; she doesn't work in the insurance industry and doesn't live in Munich. The real story wasn't about a supermarket chain as a customer. But I didn't invent what basically happened: Susan did in fact take over a sales team that was demotivated by chronic failure, focused their attention on the acquisition of new major clients – and did not let them doubt that the big fish would bite, too. From the start, her vision was as clear as her attitude: From now on we'll deliver – fast! The WhatsApp group was just one of their many new ideas. And the daily photos of team members flashing the brand of the client-to-be obviously had the desired effect. Of course, this idea wasn't the only reason why, after six years of futile acquisition attempts, things suddenly worked out so quickly. But it was a unique approach that eventually helped to turn a switch: the switch from desire to reality and from vision to implementation. The new motto now was: We think about our desired new client and their brand every day – and we will do something every day to win this client over! The emphasis here is on "daily" – not every now and then but every day!

In the end, we are not evaluated by the size of our visions but by what we put on the road. That's also why this book is called *Do Epic Stuff* – not *Think Epic Stuff*. As important as it is to have a purpose, a vision, a big goal, and as much as it helps to simulate the realization of that big goal, at a certain point it's always about delivering. You'll only do epic stuff if you're prepared to work at this point. And I mean to work *properly*! After all, we're talking about epic stuff, not about mediocre targets anyone who sits at their desks from 9 to 5 Monday through Thursday and a bit less on Fridays can achieve. Nobody will congratulate you on mediocrity. Epic stuff requires energy. Epic stuff can even mean suffering once in a while. After all, the same applies to your personal life: If you've ever set yourself the goal of building

> In the end, we are not evaluated by the size of our visions but by what we put on the road.

your own home, writing a doctoral thesis, or running a marathon, then you know that such big goals cannot be done on the side.

Granted, there are geniuses who seem to accomplish everything effortlessly that others may have to slave for. Plus, sometimes small miracles can happen when you visualize something and then it just happens without your doing and you don't even know exactly how it happened. But first of all, neither is the rule, and secondly it's not what you can take for granted. This book is not about the works of geniuses or about so-called miracles. It's about how anyone can achieve ambitious goals with his or her team. And in the end, that will – also – include work. It will include sticking with it and not giving up even when chilly winds blow in your face and things are getting uncomfortable. Many companies hire athletes as speakers, who tell their employees exciting stories about motivation, willpower, and stamina. There's nothing wrong with that. But: How many employees, who are anything but competitive athletes themselves, will then implement the recipes of top athletes in their daily work?

> Sticking with it and not giving up even when chilly winds blow in your face and things are getting uncomfortable.

I find the phrase "Where focus goes, energy flows" more helpful than the idea of super athletes as business role models. Where I put my focus in daily life, something will grow. My energy flows into what I think about all day. Brian Tracy once put it this way: "You become what you think about most of the time. The only question is: What do you think about most of the time?" If you spend many hours on Facebook or Instagram, you may increase your knowledge of how to get attention and collect likes and followers. If your goal is to become a good social media marketer, then that's okay too. If not, then the question is whether media like these really deserve so much attention. Sure: Social media can be used very well as a medium to achieve goals. Susan's WhatsApp group worked so well because it focused on one specific goal every day. Yet it was not about self-presentation and attention as an end in itself but about the focus on implementation. Media are always what we use them for.

Like Susan, you can be creative, too. Your job as Head of Epic Stuff is to make sure your people think about the epic goal more than anything else every day. It's not about cracking the whip and driving your team on. Acting like that is outdated and works increasingly less frequently. Threatening people and putting pressure on them is stupid, never sustainable, and will ultimately fall back on you in the form of stress. It's not about pressure but about aligning everyone's thinking, talking and acting on your goal and keeping it focused on a daily basis. And please don't force it; don't do it with a no-matter-what attitude but rather with serenity, optimism, and high spirits. I called this attitude "soft focus" in a previous chapter. Doggedness is never productive. The trick is to work hard every day – while staying relaxed, tolerating mistakes and not getting bogged down when something isn't working out or doesn't work as fast as you'd like. You just have to live with the fact that not everybody will always like everything you do. If you want everyone to smile at you, then you should become an ice-cream vendor.

> You just have to live with the fact that not everybody will always like everything you do. If you want everyone to smile at you, then you should become an ice-cream vendor.

The "T-Session" at a kick-off meeting is an ingenious method that lets you set the correct course at the start, clarifies what your team needs and ensures positive implementation energy. The T-Session works like this: Write that one big goal on a flipchart or a digital whiteboard. Now ask your group,"Is this our one goal? Is this what we want to achieve?" At best everyone in the room will now nod zealously. Then draw a large "T" under the goal, thus creating two columns. Write into the left column: "What we need."

And in the right column: "Why it can't work." Then cross out the right column with a large "X" and say, "I don't care about this column!" There are always a thousand reasons why something might not work. We're here to find out how it will work. It may well be that this or that may not work as desired when implementing it. But now you stop wasting your time thinking about that. If you run into real problems, your motto will be: "Change the plan, not the goal." You'll come up with something! Concentrate on what you need for the implementation in the beginning.

Now you and your team start collecting individual points until the left column is filled. With this method, you ask what your people really need so that frustration won't even build up. But beware: This method is useless if you don't deliver what your team needs! At the beginning, the energy level is always high. Utilize that initial boost of energy. Enforce what is needed to achieve your goal. Later, in the middle of implementation, it will be difficult. If the left-hand column says that everyone needs new software because the current software is not suitable – or because it doesn't really work – then make sure that this new software is purchased and installed. Once everyone has everything they need to implement, no one will have an excuse for not doing their share.

When it comes to the implementation of big goals, doer qualities are required. Some leaders hesitate at this point because they think they are strategists and their team is there for the implementation. That may basically be true. But if you don't actively get involved at the crucial moment, if you go play a round of golf at 4:30 p.m. and leave your team alone with a huge problem, then your team members won't follow you for long. Later in this chapter, I'll show you how to organize the implementation of big goals and very challenging projects in a meaningful way and what kind of personality will complement you as the Head of Epic Stuff. In everything you do it's important that you personally set an example when active involvement is required. Sure, you're not a specialist and your main task is communication – I will discuss that in the next chapter. But show at the crucial moment that you also have the qualities of a doer! Demonstrate the commitment you expect from others. As Daniel Szabo, the CEO of Körber Digital, does. In my opinion, Daniel is just the right mix: strategic, analytical and creative on the one hand – and on the other hand someone who says about himself that "Getting shit done" is his motto. I look forward to talking to Daniel about the topic of this chapter.

> Demonstrate the commitment you expect from others.

When it's time to put on gloves and rubber boots

When I meet Daniel Szabo in Berlin, he has just become CEO of the youngest division within the Körber Group: Körber Digital. Daniel's new office is located in Berlin-Mitte, bordering the Kreuzberg district and just a stone's throw away from the almost legendary "betahaus", a hotspot of the start-up scene. In the rooms of Körber Digital it looks more like a start-up than a corporation, too: There are Post-its everywhere. If a meeting room is available or taken, the only note will be a Post-it on the door. And it works! My favorite meeting room here is called "gym" and looks almost like one, too, including a punching ball and boxing gloves on the wall. While we sip delicious espressos from a semi-automatic espresso machine, Daniel and I start our conversation. Daniel joined a DAX-30 corporation with a dual degree in economics and business administration and after spending time abroad, including in China, Mexico, and Singapore. He started working in the strategy department of a business field and, after only two years, was leading the company while he was still very young. Then he managed large deals and mergers and subsequently became responsible for the issue of innovation through the transformation that was involved. Before he finally helped to establish the digitization unit of the group, he had already spent a lot of time dealing with start-up methods.

I already mentioned that Daniel is not only a strategist but also a man of action and an implementer. Pretty much the most epic proof of this is in my view that, in spite of his full-time job in the corporate world, he pulled up the start-up YOU MAWO – together with three other partners. The young company not only received many innovation awards but even became world market leader in its segment after only a few years. I want to start our conversation with that story – and then I would like to know to what extent Daniel's experiences with establishing his own company correspond to those in the corporate world. So first: What kind of company is YOU MAWO – and how come a world market leader was founded in their spare time?

"The idea came to me and three friends of mine on a beach in Thailand on one of our backpacking trips," Daniel says. "But first things first: YOU MAWO produces custom-made 3D-printed glasses. They are distributed as a high-priced premium product via the classic stationary channels of the industry. We invested only € 45,000 in the early days and have been living on cash flow ever since. After a little more than three years, we were the world leader in 3d-printed custom-made glasses and therefore a bit of a unicorn in the premium eyewear industry." As far as I know the story, it had all been decided on the beach in Thailand, hadn't it? "No, not at all. There was only this idea we had come up with. At that time, crucial patents had expired. Our question at that time on the beach was: Shouldn't we do something? I had been thinking about the eyewear industry for quite a while already because it produces huge quantities without real value added. Producing eyewear by 3D printing made perfect sense to me: It's not very expensive, and the results are as unique as the human face. A great thing! But one of us was skeptical at first, saying, 'That's nonsense,

Szabo, it's never gonna happen!' Two years later, another market player launched 3D-printed eyewear that was not custom-made, though. Then the skeptic among us reconsidered and said, 'Okay, maybe it does make sense.' Finally, when they came out with 3D scanners for iPads, with which a customer's face can be measured super easily, that was the final green light. We did some calculations and just risked it."

As far as I know, the initial phase was pretty wild? "Yes, and the company was still a pretty diffuse structure. Nevertheless, we simply registered a start-up booth at the largest German eyewear trade fair. That was in early January, a few days before the fair. Everyone had just come back from the Christmas holidays, one of us was still in India, and we had no product, no website, no marketing material, nothing. We ordered samples in six designs, but they hadn't arrived yet. We had ordered hinges, and they weren't there yet, either. Our app wasn't ready yet. So we created a few flyers overnight and made a rudimentary website. Some samples came in just before the trade fair, but a couple of them were broken. We didn't get the hinges before it was over. Besides, we still had not set any prices. Everything was close to chaos. So we sat down and said to ourselves: Okay, screw it, let's do it. We'll do it now! We just go and do our best."

> So we sat down and said to ourselves: Okay, screw it, let's do it. We'll do it now! We just go and do our best.

So everyone remembered their doer's skills and rolled up their sleeves? "Exactly! We put everything in my little car, drove to the fair, and on the way there we thought about what we should do now. I said to myself: Okay, you've studied incentive theories; we somehow have to turn the glasses into a rare product. We don't have any sales personnel, therefore the opticians will have to buy the glasses right at the fair and cannot expect a sales representative to come by later. We then put together three limited packages, each with a discount otherwise not available in the eyewear industry. Theoretically it could work. But did we dare to pull it off? Well, we finally dared it, and what happened then at the fair was totally crazy. After all, people could tell that we were unable to present a solid product. And our app still didn't work; it had a bug in it that prevented it from starting."

How did Daniel and his friends deal with the situation? "We were selling them as if our lives depended on it! Personal selling, face to face. We hit on everyone who was walking by our booth. You usually don't that in this industry. When the question of prices came up, we explained the strictly limited packages. And then things started to rock: Everybody at the trade fair quickly started to talk about YOU MAWO. After a few hours, our booth was packed. On that first day, we sold glasses for 30,000 euros. After we had invested only 5,000 euros so far. It went on like that for the next few days. Without having a presentable product! On the last day we had to stop because we knew we wouldn't get enough hinges that fast. We were sold out! At the end of the trade fair, we took a deep breath, looked at each other and said, 'Awesome what you can do if you have the right team, if you have passion and if you don't give up even under the most difficult conditions but just go and do it.'"

As far as I know, the company name YOU MAWO stands for "Your Magic World" – and this story about its founding actually has something magical about it. Especially if you consider that it took them just over three years from this impromptu fair trade appearance to become the world market leader. And no borrowed capital of even one single euro was needed for this growth. If you take a closer look, however, this wasn't magic at all but rather the exact combination of vision, positive spirit, and power to implement a goal, which is what this chapter is all about. Daniel, who has two business degrees and is a digital strategist, knew exactly when he had to roll up his sleeves, courageously become active and deliver results. I would like to know from Daniel how this mental strength can be transferred to people in larger companies. What is Daniel's advice for the Head of Epic Stuff?

"I'll start with what's been a trait I've had all my life and which I think has been a crucial factor for my success," Daniel says. "I have this *can-do* mentality and I approach issues without any bias, even in large companies. I look at how things hang together and then ask myself: Okay, what can you do here? I like to take a green-field approach and wonder what it would ideally look like. And then I say to myself: Let's just do it exactly like that! Even when there is no green field and despite all sorts of supposed hurdles. It's important not to be afraid of failure. My motto is: *Get shit done*. I imagine what it would all look like in a perfect world; then I just approach it hands-on. I'm also never afraid of doing my own thing. I like being creative and different from the norm. Particularly at the beginning of my career I met with resistance for that reason. In the end, however, I was always able to turn everything into something positive because I stuck to it. You also shouldn't be afraid to ask stupid questions. So just ask, 'Why don't we do it this way?' – even if everybody else thinks that it won't work that way. And then it's time to start!

> My motto is: *Get shit done*. I imagine what it would all look like in a perfect world; then I just approach it hands-on.

After I had just joined the corporation, I was involved in a hara-kiri project and was kicked out of the room because I had made an unusual suggestion. The gist was: 'The kid hasn't understood anything yet; he doesn't know how things work here.' Only when everything was about to fail did my bosses remember my suggestion and tried in an act of despair what I had proposed. The fact that it worked helped me a lot later, of course."

In organizations, it is quickly assumed that someone just wants to make their mark. "Exactly. That's why I always show that I'm interested in the matter. That I want to advance processes and create added value. I really do. So it's not making my mark when I say, 'Look, I sat down and prepared a proposal. Couldn't we do it this way?' I always care about the matter in hand." There are people in management who like to let others do the work and prefer to just watch. Daniel is highly intrinsically motivated and gets a lot done by himself. But how does he manage to have dozens, hundreds, perhaps even thousands of employees in a corporation follow a vision and ultimately deliver it, too?

"I let others have the same liberties I take," Daniel explains. "Everyone may ask stupid questions. Everyone may question standards. And make mistakes. That's the precondition. Moreover, I always meet people at eye level. I treat a lab assistant no differently from a board member. In concrete terms, everyone may know more about something than me. And everyone may also raise their hands and say, 'I'd like to do that my own way.' Next point: I make my visions and my enthusiasm absolutely transparent. I explain my ideas and why I think they work. I'm always empowering others as well. I say: I don't know more than you do; we're in this together. If I'm your boss, then my job is to keep your back free and shield you from flying shit. And your job is to keep things running in day-to-day operations. If it doesn't work, I won't blame you for it. Instead I'll put on gloves and rubber boots and jump into the muck heap with you, and together we'll shovel it away."

In my opinion, a head of epic stuff is exactly what Daniel has just described. If employees know that their leader has this attitude, if they get that much empowerment and trust, it will motivate them endlessly to work really hard to reach the big goal. It ensures that the implementation will succeed and the goal will become reality. Finally, I want to ask Daniel if there is anything else he wants to share. "Yes," he answers, "I just like people very much. I'm always interested in the person behind the professional. I like to talk about personal things and ask personal questions. Even if that's unusual in a corporate culture. Once I asked a board member, 'What are you doing on the weekend?' And he said, surprised, 'What do you mean?' After a while, we started talking about hobbies and interests. This is something where I'm persistent, too. By now, people are opening up more and more everywhere, and that's a good thing."

Grit in the gears may lead to a standstill

A lot of people say they want to achieve something great. Frequently, however, they already fail at the basics of implementation. In these cases, the team might not even have suitable laptops or tablets. Or they don't have company phones. Or the team members may have phones but no suitable roaming contracts in order to work globally. Or important employees from India or South Africa can't come to the kick-off because nobody thought of the visa. Believe it or not, those trifles can make your epic visions fail. So, in order to achieve your goals, you'll first of all need to take good care of your resources: people, rooms, budgets, equipment. What is important but likely to be forgotten: Is there a permanent contact point for your project, like physical headquarters? Please don't call that your "war room" – we're not at war! Words are powerful and shape your mind. So you would do better to talk about a focus room, a success room, or a launch room. Or be creative and make a narrative out of it. Maybe you're pirates on the bridge of your pirate ship – just as Christoph Hüls and his team once were. Or you might control a spaceship. Or be sitting in a rocket. What's your image?

> One of the most important basics is a team that actually has enough time to focus on the big goal.

One of the most important basics is a team that actually has enough time to focus on the big goal. When I see how a "transformation team" is formed somewhere, and Pascal is scheduled at 0.2 FTE and Lisa at 0.1 FTE, and so on until you reach 20 FTE in total, then I say: It won't work like that! Implementing epic stuff ideally means that each and every member of the team works on the subject for at least two to three hours per day. Every day! That must be your ambition. Don't let yourself be fobbed off with statements like "That's impossible!". Who is able to get up earlier and start earlier? Who can cancel meaningless meetings? Who can leave communities of practice that only hold pleasant chats? Usually more people than you think. People need enough time at a stretch to be able to focus on achieving big goals. In fact, if some people are really unable to spend time on your issue on a daily basis, then Plan B is that employees at least get some days off so they can spend several hours of time on it. What's important here is good communication: Everyone will know that Pascal and Lisa won't be available to anyone else on Thursday – because that's the day they will work exclusively for your goal.

In many cases you will need the commitment of the respective supervisors for all this. So start by making binding arrangements with the supervisors of all the people you want in your team. Then communicate the arrangements to everyone at the kick-off. In most companies this won't work without using a certain degree of hierarchical leverage. What is desired and supported "by the top" is therefore a card you may play.

> Hardly anything takes its toll faster than negligence in terms of time resources and agreements.

Hardly anything takes its toll faster than negligence in terms of time resources and agreements. Nowadays, employees in large companies are burdened with way too many tasks from all sides. Without agreements that are binding and have been communicated clearly, the focus will be lost – and therefore the most important precondition for success!

At this point I again want to return to the issue of one goal: There is always just one big goal, never several goals simultaneously. You should remind yourself of that fact over and over again on your way to the goal. A common mistake: The big goal is announced, you start with lots of momentum – and all too soon this project and that project will be added, and all these other projects will require a lot of attention. With every new project that's announced somewhere, it's your job to make it clear to everyone involved that the one goal still is your No. 1 Priority. Keep in mind that people's level of attention is always high when something is new and unusual. So, if you notice that there is a new project elsewhere that your people find fascinating, explicitly ask for prioritization. If necessary, with the support of their superiors, too. So that everyone in the team will know what they're going the extra mile for: that one big goal that won't be jeopardized in any way.

If you have your people together and you have your resources, if everyone has enough time and everybody's focus is on the big goal, then you can finally make sure that everyone has free rein in their daily work and doesn't constantly waste time on annoying little things that only affect their focus. The proverbial grit in the gears slows everything down more and more. It may at first not look like a major problem if someone is constantly leaving the office to buy coffee because the job of the person who used to take care of the coffee supply was cut. Or if someone is constantly booking their flights and hotels on booking portals because they don't have an assistant for that. Or if someone sorts receipts for half an hour and numbers them by date.

If you add it up, however, such trifles will distract people from their focus and can slow down the implementation of your goal enormously. Which brings us to the annoying issue of saving money in the wrong place. If the office that handles travel expenses figures that it will save the company money if the employees have to travel three-quarters of an hour extra twice so as to spend the night in a cheap hotel, then you must make them understand that this calculation is wrong. The same applies if certain employees are not authorized to take a taxicab. Or if assistant jobs are dropped because in the digital age everyone can do everything themselves anyway. Yes, of course they can. But is their time and energy used effectively? Some things that look like superfluous luxuries to jealous colleagues or penny pinchers simply serve to reduce time and energy losses, eliminate annoying disturbances, and thereby keep people's concentration on a high level. That's the reason for that taxi ride, for the more expensive hotel right at the terminal of the airport. Focus is always the most important thing – and anything that improves people's focus will pay off in the long run. This issue may lead to conflicts you will then just have to solve. The goal is always: the optimum empowerment of everyone involved.

Before I address the issue of the distribution of roles on your way to the big goal in detail, I would like to talk to another person who might have invented the motto "Go big or stay home" himself. While, to me, Daniel Szabo is like a young skydiver, for the second conversation in this chapter I deliberately chose someone whose perspective on things is enriched with an unusual amount of experience. My conversation with Joachim Jäckle – he will be retired by the time this book is published – takes place shortly before his 6oth birthday, a time when the top manager looks back on one half of a lifetime working for Henkel. 30 years in the same company is a very long time – how does one manage to be successful again and again over this long period while motivating others to contribute to the success, too? With these questions in mind, I'm on my way to Henkel's headquarters in Dusseldorf to meet the CIO and Global Head of Integrated Business Solutions of this globally active consumer goods corporation.

Where change is a daily thing, you need flexibility for the implementation of goals

I must admit I had pictured a different work environment of a CIO in a company that is more than 140 years old: Joachim Jäckle sits among many other employees. Everything here is open plan; the boss's desk is no exception. Art is important to Joachim Jäckle, as you can see in every corner: Items from the Henkel art collection adorn the walls – here and in other buildings of the company headquarters. "Art helps to be creative," he says. "I also consider the fact that we have works of art everywhere to be a form of appreciation for the people who work here." After Joachim Jäckle briefly showed me the spectacular view over the extensive premises of the Henkel headquarters in Dusseldorf, we withdraw to one of the "focus rooms". Unlike the busy open office space, this room is a peaceful haven. Here we can focus fully on our conversation. Before talking about the actual issue of how people are motivated by big goals, we talk a little about goals per se. Even for Joachim Jäckle, not "change" but "goals" are the basis for everything. More precisely: goal setting and acceptance of the goal. The experienced manager obviously doesn't think much of actionism.

"Before concentrating on the implementation," Joachim Jäckle says, "I must have sufficiently dealt with the question of what the goal that I want to achieve and communicate really is. I see a major change here that has occurred over the past three decades: In the past, it often sufficed if supervisors – from department heads to board members – defined top-down goals that the company should achieve. All this was unquestionably accepted until a few years ago. Today things are different: It's no longer just about the goal itself but also about how to formulate the goal. And the goal must be realistic; at the same time it should be ambitious. Most of the people I know want to work on a big goal."

That's why the book for which we are having this conversation is called *Do Epic Stuff*. Today, if you want to have the best people in your team, you have to give them the chance to achieve big goals. "I'm certainly exaggerating a bit in terms of language when I say that it's about helping to make this world a better place. In companies, too, motivation arises from the idea of making a positive contribution that goes beyond your own area," Joachim Jäckle says. "Here at Henkel, for example, sustainability plays a major role. Today, I have to be able to formulate goals that contain value components. And in a way that lets people consciously decide to participate. In plain terms: It is not God-given that employees work for me as a manager or for Henkel. I have to earn that decision again and again as a company and as a supervisor. That's the big difference from 30 years ago, when I started here. I have to consider greater things today. Sustainability and environmental issues are a good example, but not the only one. As a company, we are part of society. And just as society is constantly changing, so are we."

That also affects our daily working life. We work differently today than we did 30 years ago. Methods that still worked then don't work today. This particularly applies to change management. But also to the organization of work. "We come from a division of labor: There are several departments that specialize in certain sections of a process or are part of a larger task. In order to achieve great goals together and then continue being successful, we must first overcome the hurdles of the division of labor. That means that all employees can see as much of the picture as possible, the *big picture*. Everybody should have an overall understanding of what we're doing here – and why we're doing it. This is not limited to what your own workplace means in a narrower sense. But everyone should also understand what happens to the results of his or her work, what effect it has on the big picture. In the past, there was less emphasis put on that. Today, I don't only have to understand that but also take responsibility for it. It also requires a high degree of proactivity: I can't wait until something is explained to me but rather have to actively acquire the knowledge myself – as a company we have to create the right platforms and offers. It's about ownership on the individual level with a view of the whole picture. In my opinion, this is crucial if you want to master demanding projects and realize great visions today."

If this is the new framework, and if a company succeeds in creating it and making sure that people really want to work there, the question is still how to practically get my employees actually to do their share. What are the challenges from Joachim Jäckle's viewpoint? How does he realize that people get the big picture, that they see themselves as part of it – and then take responsibility, stay focused, and work towards the ultimate goal every day? And what is different here, too, today?

"Today's practice is completely different than it used to be," Joachim Jäckle says. "In the past, there were isolated change projects – I don't want to use the term 'patchwork' but that's pretty much how you can picture it. For example, they introduced software that adapted processes, trained employees, created acceptance, and then things would stay the same for a few more years. Today the world works differently. Things are changing continuously and much faster than before. For example, today we have evergreen concepts for software where the manufacturer changes things almost every week. There are no more standstills or breaks – instead, you keep adapting to new conditions. The decision to change comes from outside the company; the market and the customers set the pace. This can be transferred to work in general. Today, performance also means constantly changing with the environment: I undergo continuous processes of change and will have to be able to deal with new requirements in two weeks that today I don't know yet."

I like to use the formula: *Change the plan, not the goal*. The focus remains on the big goal, while I must adapt to its implementation again and again. "This is also reflected in the project management and the new procedures we use, for instance *Scrum* or *DevOps*," Joachim Jäckle says. "In doing so, you continually redefine the priorities and don't even specify everything down to the last detail at first. Today we can be more adventurous because we can also readjust better. If I change a priority in a project today and try something new, I will be able to see at the next touchpoint in two weeks if it was useful or not – and correct it accordingly. That requires openness, flexibility – and the willingness to continuously learn and to admit that something didn't work out as planned."

You can tell that Joachim Jäckle's approach is shaped by the IT world. Nevertheless, I believe that the changes in the daily work on big goals that he describes will ultimately affect the whole working world. This is already evident in the change in working environments you can see everywhere today. That's why I explicitly address the environment in which our conversation takes place at the headquarters of Henkel.

"We totally believe in our open space and the whole new workplace concept, including digital applications such as Skype or Office 365, which we use extensively. These technologies have significantly improved our collaboration. Screen sharing or flexible desks were unthinkable here a few years ago; today they're indispensable for our organization. I've also decided to do without an office of my own to set a good example. It was a great experience for me. It helps me to be much better informed about what's going on. It inspires me to walk through the corridors more often. When I see that somebody is around, I just walk over there instead of writing a formal email. People talk to me directly more frequently than they used to. We also have special rooms people can use when they need to retreat. However, openness means much more than open space with the same workplaces for everyone. You also need to create platforms and new formats that allow people to openly address issues and talk about where things are going. Not everyone has the courage to do that right away. A new culture of trust is needed, and it must grow first. It's a development process."

What kind of new formats are these? Joachim Jäckle gives me some examples: "We started a series of events inspired by the so-called *fuck-up nights* and the start-up world. True to the motto 'Sometimes you win, sometimes you learn', executives talk about failed projects. That's very popular! It creates the trust that you can speak openly about problems at any time. In the past, people were always afraid of damaging their careers. The key idea today is: It's not about sharing failures but about learning. Our global IBS town halls, where all employees worldwide can participate, either on-site or by Skype, are another example. We use different digital tools and therefore create a totally different kind of communication: In the past it was always bad if the boss talked for an hour and there was no interaction. Today employees can comment – even anonymously – on anything that has been said in live chats – and the whole world watches it! At first, some people thought that anyone could air their frustration without being identified, and then it would be visible on a huge screen. But such fears are unfounded. Of course, there are times when someone tries to be a bit provocative. But that must be possible, and it's best if I, as their leader, handle that with a sense of humour."

At the end of my conversation with Joachim Jäckle, I'm interested in whether there are any situations in the IT sector at Henkel where everyone shows their macho qualities, rolls up their sleeves and really does everything to go that extra mile. "Most definitely," Joachim Jäckle replies promptly. "I'm proud to have a very dedicated team. This is evident both in day-to-day business operations and in projects. Of course there are situations that are special – and I'm not just talking about critical issues, such as defending the company against cyber attacks. It also shows up in hot project phases. Then it no longer matters who has what role or position. It's about finding solutions and working together to make the project a success. These are those goosebump moments that end up giving me energy in the end, too."

Your congenial support: from PMO to TMO

In the previous world of change management and project management, there was the project manager on the one hand – and on the other hand, complementing that role, there was the project management officer (PMO) as head of the project management office. The PMO took care of everything organizational, especially the project plans and deadlines. He or she made meetings happen and made sure everyone in the team had access to resources at all times. According to these tasks, a PMO's typical personality profile was: objective and organized, diligent and conscientious, a pronounced sense of practicality as well as strong nerves. Up to now, PMOs frequently used to be taciturn stoics who did their jobs inconspicuously; they were as reliable as a Swiss watch. No question: As the head of epic stuff you'll need people with these skills in the future, too. As you develop and communicate your vision, never tire of telling your story in the company, present your goals to executives, secure the necessary budgets and do everything to ensure the team has the right focus and motivation, another team member will take over the responsibility for your daily needs.

So what's new? To do epic stuff, it's no longer enough to have a traditional PMO at your side. Besides having a talent for organizing, a person who congenially complements you as the head of epic stuff must now be able to score points in communication. He or she takes care of practical matters, covers your back – and at the same time spreads your great vision. He or she acts in a well-structured and reliable

> To do epic stuff, it no longer suffices to have a traditional PMO at your side.

manner – while being empathetic and appreciative towards everyone in the team. You may be able to communicate your vision in a way that thrills your listeners more – but, if necessary, your "Number 2" will be able convey it, too. For you, focus, motivation and inspiration are the most important things – but they also matter to your congenial addition in the organizational area. I call this new role TMO – for *transformation management officer*. Accordingly, the old project management office for change projects becomes the transformation management office. Modifying terms must never be an end in itself; I will discuss this in more detail in the next chapter. For me, this is about real change and an extension of the previous understanding of roles and not just a new term.

It is also important for big goals that an inspired focus is created, sustained and brought into the business for it to be exclusively your responsibility as head of epic stuff. Your "Number 2" may support you as much as possible in this matter. What distinguishes you from the TMO is, above all, the weighting: you are responsible for vision, inspiration and communication – but as soon as the implementation becomes challenging, you also show your hands-on abilities. Conversely, the TMO's job is primarily hands-on. But if the focus threatens to weaken and people's motivation collapse at times, this person will also know how to inspire the team and sharpen its focus. Does that make the role of TMO an allrounder? No, because just as entire departments are now changing from silos to agile entities, so are the demands on individuals. Today, people get to be more versatile than before, and in addition to their primary role, they also have one or more secondary roles.

If you look around in today's working world, you'll soon find that things look similar everywhere: Previously, the phone company technician would come to your home and install your new telephone socket without saying a word. Today he's also a sales representative, who will advise you on new products and is trained to take advantage of opportunities for upselling. For a taxi driver, it was once enough to be able to operate a car. Today, if he's not friendly and well-mannered, if he doesn't help you with your luggage and doesn't know how to take care of a car and keep it clean, he will hardly get 5-star reviews through his passengers' mobility apps. For a long time, flight attendants have naturally been assuming the dual role of service staff and safety officers in emergencies. Today, even police officers are expected to handle more tasks than regulating traffic and chasing criminals: They are supposed to be friendly, to assist citizens and represent the democratic constitutional state, communicate skillfully, act reassuringly and de-escalating, and prevent problems from occuring, if possible. In every field, professional roles are becoming ever more complex and multi-layered. And almost everywhere good communication skills are part of today's job profiles.

As head of epic stuff, you are primarily responsible for good communication. You talk about the epic goal every day and keep the team focused on it. However, you're not alone with this task. Others support you, especially your "Number 2", the man or woman for organizational matters. Together you get your vision on the road.

Here is a short and concise overview of the entire process – from vision to achievement of goals:

1. Define your epic goal: one goal, not multiple goals!
2. Break the big goal into manageable smaller packages: slicing
3. Define leads: Who do you need to reach your goal?
4. Find a TMO for organization and communication
5. Put your project team together across traditional boundaries
6. Reserve a physical room as your headquarters and contact point
7. Create your simulation of the day you reach your goal ("the future in 4D")
8. Ensure a phenomenal start using the simulation
9. Work hard with everyone on the big goal daily and keep them focused on it
10. Talk about the epic goal every day and keep telling your story
11. Back up your team and demand that the goal has priority over any new projects
12. Party hard with your team when your goal is achieved.

No matter at what point of the process you're right now: Everywhere, good communication is the be-all and end-all. Classical change and innovation projects have already shown: If project managers were asked at the end what they wished they had done better while working on their project, the most important point was usually: to communicate more and better! Various surveys have been showing that. But what *is* good and correct communication? Sure: You want to transport your message. But why is that often so hard to do? And how can you ensure that you'll manage to in the future? You will find answers to these questions in the next chapter.

Chapter 8

Explain It to a 7-Year-Old: Simple Communication

When Julian came to breakfast at the Empire Plaza Resort & Conference Center, the buffet had already been pretty much ransacked: a silver plate with some left-over slices of cheese, a glass bowl with a few sorry-looking chunks of fruit soaked in fruit juice, all framed by slices of not-so-popular breads. The tables in the dining room were hardly any more inviting: everywhere he looked there were used coffee cups and plates with leftovers. The air was so stuffy that it seemed to be telling him to run away. Julian was late. His nearly three hundred colleagues at the pharmaceutical company seemed to have attacked the buffet like a swarm of locusts. Now they had moved on to the room named "London", where the presentation of a groundbreaking new drug was to start in nine minutes.

Julian, the young social media manager, would never have volunteered for presentations like this one. Wasn't it enough if the pharmaceutical representatives, most of whom had a scientific background, listened to these dry lectures? But Julian's boss had insisted on his attendance. First-hand information was important, he had said. And that it was always about networking, too. So what could Julian have done? Usually he tried to combine such appointments with something nice. The evening before he had met Erik, his former fellow student who had just founded a chatbot start-up. Later that night, Erik had wanted to show Julian his favorite bar. Julian had finally been dropped off by a taxicab outside the Empire Plaza at 2:20 a. m.

The hotel staff hurriedly cleared the tables, wiped them clean and refilled the buffet. But they couldn't do miracles. No great progress was to be expected within the next five minutes. Julian pushed the button for a double espresso on a WMF coffeemaker and grabbed a banana. Even a 28-euro breakfast could look like that. After he had sat down at one of the clean tables, he took the information brochure for the new drug out of his backpack. Maybe he could use the waiting time to go through some of the material? Julian opened the brochure. After a few pages of pretty but meaningless photos, he found a short introductory text and began to read:

> Bamulevar is a fully human, monoclonal antibody from the immuno-checkpoint inhibitor class used in oncological immunotherapy. Bamulevar specifically connects with the programmed ligands PD-L1 (corresponds to CD274, B7 homologous with 1). This ensures the prevention from its connecting with its receptor PD-1. A PD-1/PD-L1 receptor/ligand interaction leads to the inhibition of CD8 + T cells and thus to the inhibition of the immune defence. Immunotherapy with Bamulevar aims to lift this inhibition by controlling the interaction of receptor and ligand ...

Had he really closed his eyes? Julian put the booklet aside and took a bite of his banana. That very moment David, Julian's e-commerce colleague, walked past his table. He was heading for the conference hall in a hurry. "Hey, Julian!" David said. "Still eating breakfast? It's starting in two minutes." Julian got up, took the booklet in one hand and picked up his backpack with his other hand. "Hey, David, I'm coming, too." Julian knew that David had also been forced to attend these presentations. That was why he didn't beat around the bush: "I just tried to start reading the material and gave up. I hope Dr. Frenzel-Schweickhardt isn't doing the presentation again because then I'll fall asleep in my chair." The two of them reached the room and looked for the last empty seats in the back. "I've heard that a newbie's giving the presentation today," David said. "Someone our age." Julian was surprised: "Oh, really?" They found two empty seats right next to each other.

The lights on the empty stage were dimmed. Trippy electronic music sounded from concealed speakers. Noah entered the stage from the right side – dressed in jeans, sneakers, an orange polo shirt and a blue blazer that fit him perfectly. At that moment, a huge picture of Harry Potter, dressed in his cloak of invisibility embellished with magical symbols, appeared on the screen behind him. Noah slowly walked to the centre of the stage. Without a word of greeting, he immediately started with his story:

> Imagine you are the good proteins and want to strengthen the healthy cells for the battle against the dark Lord Cancer and his evil helpers. But the dark forces are just everywhere! The fight seems hopeless. As soon as you approach Lord Cancer, his helpers recognize you, jump on you and chase you away. What if you had a cloak of invisibility now? Like Harry Potter's robe? Then you could approach Lord Cancer unrecognized by his henchmen and secretly get to the healthy cells. We have this camouflage cape now! I came here to present it. Its name is Bamulevar.

"Wow," Julian whispered to David. "Now I know what Bamulevar is." David nodded. "Even our youngest son would have understood what our new colleague has just said up there. And he turned seven last week."

When nobody understands anything but everybody looks satisfied …

No epic stuff without focused, inspirational communication! If you don't get your message transported, you might as well forget the rest. And if you don't remind your crew of your big goal every day, then the focus will soon be lost. Communication is not just important – communication is essential! When I say that in large companies with these or similar words – at the abstract level, that is – everyone nods in agreement. Then they get up and continue with the normal insanity of daily communication in the corporate world. This common kind of communication reminds me of the two varieties of bad chili: Either the chili is not spicy enough and tastes bland. In a company that means: People are only jabbering without getting to the point. The spices in the form of key messages you can write down and remember are missing. But bad chili can also be too spicy; then your stomach and intestines can't digest it. That means: People are throwing details at you as if there were no tomorrow. Then you get to see 150 slides in the space of thirty minutes, and each slide is packed with text, numbers and graphics. This will make you feel like you've just spent a weekend binge-watching trash TV: Nothing will stick.

One thing makes everything even more complicated – and stranger: Hardly anyone intervenes if the communication is poor. When does someone ever ask, "Could we please get to the point now?" Or: "So what does that mean in concrete terms?" Or ask for an example so that he or she can better understand a situation. Or admit frankly, "I didn't get that!" Instead, there is a fatal mix of "live and let live" and the fear of losing face. The agreement seems to be: I won't ask you any critical questions now – and you'll leave me alone the next time, too. No one will interrupt and ask for an explanation even if they are confronted with the most exotic terms or most obscure abbreviations. Who knows, perhaps I just didn't pay any attention when it was explained. All of the others may know what SGBMM stands for. I'm the only one who doesn't know, and it would embarrass me if that came to light. Perhaps the person who is doing the presentation right now was just too lazy to spell out "Senior Global Brand Marketing Manager" on her slide. I can only guess what the abbreviation is supposed to mean.

A culture of sometimes redundant, sometimes overly detailed communication, combined with the ubiquitous fear of losing face, is the ideal breeding ground for all kinds of linguistic excesses. How easy is it to hide behind all kinds of technical terms, abbreviations and acronyms? Or behind a grotesque jargon of business terms and marketing vocabulary? Only too easy. For that reason, many people can obviously not resist the temptation. Yet the old rule that anyone who has really grasped his or her subject can present the context in a simple way still applies. A complicated way of expressing yourself is often an obvious indication of only superficial knowledge. The poet Johann Wolfgang von Goethe once put it this way: "Dirt that we tread isn't hardened but spread." Goethe would probably be surprised how much dirt is being spread in large companies today. Who in the corporate world (another beautiful term!) doesn't feel a bit guilty when reading these sentences? Not that I want to deny that I'm guilty, too. So how can we communicate better?

> A complicated way of expressing yourself is often an obvious indication of only superficial knowledge.

First of all, we may all realize that knowledge and information are the most important commodities in large organizations today. People handle everything that is valuable and important with care. So we have every reason to be careful with knowledge and information. Language is the most important medium for transmitting knowledge and information – it's even more important than numbers or graphics, which rarely make sense if they're not embedded in a linguistic context. So we must also handle our language carefully. People who don't pay attention to their language, don't pay much attention to their thoughts – and, in the end, not to their actions, either. The issue of the congruence between personality and statement will be discussed later in this chapter.

> People who don't pay attention to their language, don't pay much attention to their thoughts and, in the end, not to their actions, either.

The next thing is that – at least in my world – an expert is someone who can explain complicated things in simple language. Nobody needs professionals who make complicated topics even more complicated linguistically. Incomprehensible, abstract talk will put listeners in a trance. Incidentally, hypnosis actually works like this! A hypnotist slowly lulls you in with abstract sentences. So ask yourself: Do I want to hypnotize people or do I want to bring my message across? For example, when a steering committee meets, members typically want to get the quick picture. Smoke and mirrors won't help anyone here. Or, if a CEO has 15 minutes to understand an issue and then decide whether or not to support the issue in question, every second that doesn't transport a message, any image or storytelling will be a waste of his time. The best motto for situations like these is: Explain it in a way that any 7-year-old could understand. For that guarantees that the control committee, the CEO, the investor, the shareholders, and so on will understand it.

> Incomprehensible, abstract talk will put listeners in a trance.

Finally, the third and last rule for me is never to merely fiddle with language without really changing the underlying ways of thinking, the concepts, structures and processes. I'm not talking primarily about the language of so-called political correctness, which is a topic on its own. What I mean is that certain buzzwords find their way into companies and are then adopted – and that, except the language, nothing much will change. The result is old wine in new bottles. Allegedly everybody works "flexibly", and instead of an organization chart you will only have "tribes" and "chapters" and "squads". The project manager is now the "scrum master" – yet still does 99 per cent of the same work as last year. In that type of situation the employees don't work on epic goals but only learn new vocabulary. A modified language is supposed to simulate a cultural change that in reality is not taking place. First of all, improve the culture, structures and processes, and then consider whether new terms make any sense – and if so, which ones. I'd rather have a "department" that puts epic stuff on the road than a "tribe" that spends half the day toying with plastic words. Do experts feel the way I do? In Frankfurt I get on a train to talk to a communications pro.

The art of leaving out the fat and getting to the point

I'm sitting in the ICE with Axel Löber, Head of Global Brand & Marketing of the German energy corporation E.ON. We're heading towards Essen. The Easter holidays have just started and the train is packed. Passengers are pushing and shoving each other; travelers who didn't reserve a seat are sitting on the floor or standing in the aisle. Everybody's talking at the same time. If we manage to focus on the essence of our conversation here on this train, then we're actually doing what the subject of this chapter is about! Axel is an out and out communication pro. He knows the subject of communication from the different perspectives of the consulting world and the corporate world. After studying German, politics and psychology, he learned the basics of his trade at a small PR agency: press releases, copy texts, catchy headlines. This was followed by a stint in Germany's leading strategic communications consulting firm. His next station was the world of large corporations: The communications of the finance section and the board were stepping stones on his way to brand management – "it just fell into my lap," he says. At Merck, he eventually oversaw the global brand and, in his own words, "rebuilt it a bit". That's the understatement of the year. Merck's radically transformed brand identity has not only been an iconic transformation for the 350-year-old science and technology company but has also amazed people way beyond the industry. I still have to smile when I recall a business show on CNN where a journalist visited the new Merck website live at the studio. With wide-open eyes, he shouted, "Gosh, that looks like an Austin Powers movie!" Well, Axel knows other colours besides dark blue and other forms than just the right angle.

Even though Axel, now that he works for E.ON, sticks to the issue of brand, our talk today is not about branding but about communication. And first I want to confess that, being a person who does not have a communications background, I learned a lot from Axel. I automatically associate the phrase "Take the jellyfish fat out of this" with him. Our discussions about texts have made me aware of many linguistic subtleties. I want to start with a general question: What, in Axel's opinion, is simple communication? "For me, the key is to find out what moves my dialogue partner and how to make an emotional and intellectual connection.

> I can understand, remember and reproduce what is simple and visually tangible.

After all, communication is not a one-way street," Axel said. "It's important to get to the core of the issue and to word it concisely. The world is already complex enough. If we explain things in even more complicated terms, they will be even harder to grasp or even not get through the medial white noise. Incidentally, I don't think that's a phenomenon of our time. We live in the VUCA world, that's correct. But there has always been complexity – and the simple truths that made this world accessible to us. Great myths as well as my grandmother's home-spun wisdom. I can understand, remember and reproduce what is simple and visually tangible."

That sounds sensible. When I look at organizations, I notice one of the biggest problems is that the communication is either too long-winded or too complicated. Nevertheless, a CEO who gets thousands of pieces of information on his desk every day is supposed to listen to me, despite the fact that on his last trip to the lavatory he already met three other employees who were all trying to talk his ears off. And at the same time, each of them also wanted to emphasize their expert status. Yet I still want my ten minutes of attention without coming across as an idiot. So how do I do that? "First of all, it has to have something to do with what's actually on your conversation partner's mind," explains Axel. "Everyone has their agenda and certain issues on their desk. If what you say is not related to that at this moment, then it's not relevant for them. The second thing I do is to reduce my communication to essentials: What's the essential information your counterpart should be getting? What does he or she have to know – and what don't they need to know? To get there, you take the jellyfish fat out. This phrase was coined by the former German chancellor, Helmut Schmidt. Don Draper from *Mad Men* put it like this: 'Keep it simple but significant.' That's exactly it. A message must be relevant and significant, and it must be an argument that's simple enough in the already complex working world. So how do I get there? It's important not to lose yourself in details. In the first step, I focus on the core information and convey it as succinctly as possible. I let the details follow in the second step – or even let someone else deliver them later. Carving out the core idea is the hardest part. There's a certain truth in the saying 'I'll write you a long letter because I don't have the time for a short one'."

What can people use to guide them if they just want to communicate? Does Axel have any examples or advice? "I like the children's TV show *Die Sendung mit der Maus*," says Axel. "In professional contexts, I've often recommended to let yourself be guided by non-fiction stories." Internationally, the feature "Big Bird learns about ..." in *Sesame Street* may be better known. "Exactly. The programme itself isn't all that important; I'm talking about explanatory films for children as inspiration. That's how we can learn to get things across easily. Ask yourself: How would you explain something to a 5-year-old? Or your grandmother, who has no idea about the subject? If you can do that, then you hold the key in your hand. Always communicate as if your recipients were not professionals but laypeople. If they are professionals, they will be generally happy about someone who puts their complicated profession into a catchy phrase. Of course, you should be prepared to answer questions about detail issues. Consider a good management template, for example: It has a headline that's to the point, contains an executive summary that includes the essence and then 10 pages of details. If the headline doesn't get the reader's attention and if the executive summary doesn't pinpoint the facts, the 10 pages of details are for nothing."

> How would you explain something to a 5-year-old? Or your grandmother, who has no idea about the subject? If you can do that, then you hold the key in your hand.

When reading executive summaries, I would sometimes like to ask: Could I get a summary of this summary, please? Even the summaries are often too bloated for my liking. Or take PowerPoint slides. Actually, they force you to concentrate, but some people manage to overload a slide with information so that the core is already forgotten again. "Absolutely. There's this famous memo Winston Churchill wrote during the air war with Germany. In his memo, the Prime Minister requests all members of the War Cabinet to cut things short as of right now, because otherwise they would waste too much energy and couldn't think clearly. Even though we're riding a train right now, let's think about a sports car. It's light and agile. You have to slam the steering wheel of a heavy car around bends, so you never get the sports car feeling with it. It is the same with communication: You can only make yourself clear if your statement is clear. What is concise and – ideally – differentiating is easy to remember. That's why claims work so well: 'Just do it', 'Think different', 'Only the best or nothing at all'. A whole corporate philosophy is being broken down to a few words. That's enough to convey an idea, and sometimes it says as much as 150 pages or a website. Ultimately, this is exactly what branding is all about: defining the core idea of your company or product."

During the time he was responsible for a CEO's communication, Axel also wrote speeches. Frankly, I find that many speeches make me fall asleep. How do you write a speech that will keep people awake? "First you research the topic, and then you structure the contents. Then you write the speech. But the main work, the work that is by far the most time-consuming, comes in the end: The speech needs to be put into its final form – and that means cutting the text down to the bones. Even if something has been painstakingly researched and worded, it may be necessary to delete it. That's the jellyfish fat. Abraham Lincoln's Gettysburg Address consisted of only 272 words. Even today, it's still one

> Conciseness brings clarity.

of the most important speeches in American history. It takes less than three minutes to say 272 words. Can I remember any of the 30-minute speeches from any conference? Not a single one. Somebody could talk for an hour; it wouldn't make a difference. I wouldn't remember it anyway. But three minutes might make a difference. Conciseness brings clarity. "

Does Axel have any final piece of advice? "Twitter makes for a nice exercise," he says. "You have only 280 characters. If I want to make my point with these few letters, every word must matter. Donald Trump manages to communicate his politics via Twitter. That's an art. Without passing judgement on the content: Just look at the effect it has." Compared to that, the two of us us have talked quite a bit already. But now to the point. "I think everything I've just told you could've been said in just four sentences," Axel says, straightening his colourful tie. Okay, I still want to write a book people like to read, and not just a note. But then a book is exactly that level of detail Axel has just described. If the essence is clear, then the level of detail has its justification, too.

Facts are vulnerable, stories are not

Some time ago, a well-established major publishing house that had been publishing newspapers, magazines, and books for decades founded a digital media subsidiary. It took almost a whole year to find a suitable managing director for the new digital division. However, the publishing house didn't want to wait that long to build up the staff of its subsidiary. After just a few weeks, a young team started to work on its first digital projects. The team was to cooperate with the employees of the parent company and also obtain contents from them. The CFO of the publishing house was appointed acting director. He looked at the numbers from time to time and otherwise stayed out of it. When Jeff came along, they finally had the managing director they had been longing for. Although he was a newcomer to the publishing industry, he had a lot of experience with digital business models. He also had already managed large departments in corporations. For the first few days and weeks, Jeff was thrilled that his new team members had organized themselves so well. They seemed to be already pursuing exciting projects. That suited Jeff's mentality, which was to inspire and motivate his workers rather than giving them any specific subjects to work on. However, Jeff soon noticed that something was wrong.

The cooperation of the young digital team with the employees of the established publisher didn't work at all. When Jeff asked his team members what was going on, they reported, "We have no idea why they're acting the way they do. They're supposed to support us, but they don't." Jeff asked the staff of the publishing house about their views of his new team. The message was clear: "They're conceited; they're cocky artists who think they've reinvented the wheel with their digital equipment without having earned a single euro yet. But still they're getting all the money while we're supposed to save money." Jeff started to watch his team carefully for the next few weeks. Yes, there were some great ideas for exciting projects. But not much was actually realized. The little that the parent company saw was poorly researched, sloppy, and flawed. At the same time, everybody was complaining about not having enough money to do something great. So Jeff rounded up his team members and told them the following story:

> "Imagine you are a hyped-up young chef who opens a gourmet restaurant. Your recipes are awesome. And you've found a great location. Your first guests come into your restaurant and look forward to having a great evening. They're looking forward to your innovative cuisine. But then the waiter ignores them. They have to seat themselves. All the tablecloths are dirty. When the waiter does come to their table, he looks grim and doesn't say much. The meals on the menu he hands out are much too expensive. He's unable to recommend wine to go with the meal. Instead, the guests have to say which wine they want to drink. When the food finally arrives after ninety minutes, it's almost cold and too salty. Though your recipes are exquisite, you're not concentrating on cooking the meals in the kitchen. The guests are annoyed and ask for the bill. It's incorrect – 40 euros too much. When the guests complain that this restaurant is terrible and not even the basics were OK, the waiter only says, 'I don't know what you're talking about. Our boss is a genius. We should be charging much higher prices; that's our only problem.'"

After Jeff had told this story, he left the room. Embarrassed, the team members looked down. Nobody said a word.

This didn't actually happen in a publishing house, but my story is based on a true story in another industry. By telling stories, the new managing director has mastered the difficult task of holding up a mirror to his team. Without any accusations and without endless discussions where no one wants to give in. Storytelling works. The beauty of a story is that it can't be refuted. Facts are vulnerable, stories are not. Well, you may doubt if the story is a suitable analogy for a certain situation. But that's another story. First, it's just a story. Narratives always touch people at the emotional level first and then at the rational level. For the historian Yuval Noah Harari, stories are even the glue that holds every human society together: "Any human endeavor on a large scale … is firmly rooted in common stories that exist only in people's minds," Harari writes in his bestseller *A Brief History of Humankind*.

Stories, metaphors, analogies, and linguistic imagery are a must when it comes to simple communication. The saying "A picture is worth a thousand words" also applies to linguistic images. When Julian, a young social media manager in a pharmaceutical company, reads the scientific description of the new drug "Bamulevar", he doesn't understand a single word. But when Noah later explains the effect of "Bamulevar" by using the image of Harry Potter's cloak of invisibility and telling a little story, Julian immediately grasps what it's all about. Incidentally, I didn't invent the scientific description I quoted, even though it may sound like satire to pharmacological laymen. It is based on a Wikipedia article about a real substance used in oncology. And the comparison with Harry Potter was mentioned in a lecture on this drug I attended. The speaker totally impressed me by doing

> Stories, metaphors, analogies, and linguistic imagery are a must when it comes to simple communication.

that! At the time I thought that it's really simple to bring any highly complicated subject matter across by using a catchy image and a story that even a 7-year-old will understand.

The 5C principle of simple and authentic communication

If you want to do epic stuff, you always have to think about how to communicate with others as simply as possible in order to be understood. Simple, clear language makes it easier for your team members to focus. Make sure that what you say answers the so-called "wh-questions": What are we doing? Who does it? Where do we do it? How do we do it? Why are we doing it? By checking whether your statements respond to wh-questions, you make sure that you're communicating content – and are not just fooling around. As a leader, you should always communicate authentically. Save money on rhetoric seminars that will teach you something that doesn't suit your personality. People subconsciously notice whether words or gestures are not authentic, and they find a person who communicates as if he or she was trained to speak not to be credible. With some executives, you can literally see which kinds of rhetorical training they underwent. When they talk or do a presentation, they act like puppets. Instead deal with the principles of good communication – and then implement them in your own way. What does simplicity mean to you? What form of storytelling is right for you? Someone will tell a story in five minutes; someone else will tell the same story in one sentence. Both are okay as long as it's authentic.

No matter what style suits your personality best, your communication should always be clear, congruent, concrete, consistent, and contextualized. That's the 5C principle of good communication. What does it mean exactly?

- **Clarity** is the opposite of the notorious smoke candles. Clear communication is reduced, simple and graphic. It avoids incomprehensible terminology and unnecessary abbreviations (such as GBM for "global brand marketing" or ASAP for "as soon as possible"). Clarity does not necessarily always mean brevity. At the detail level, your statements may be detailed. What matter is that every sentence contains a statement.

- **Congruence** means that your statements agree with both the facts you know and your own personality. People can sense acutely whether or not you believe in what you're saying. They also sense if you've rehearsed any sentences or body language just for effect. So be authentic in a professional way and just talk about what you really believe.

- **Concrete** is the opposite of abstract and means communication that clearly states facts and works with comprehensible examples, images, and stories. People who remain only on the abstract level will quickly lose their listeners' attention. They will also raise their listeners' suspicion that they have something to hide. Concrete communication always includes answers to wh-questions (what, who, where, how, why?).

- **Consistency** means that your statements are free from any contradictions. There are speakers who constantly contradict themselves in a single lecture. They usually have not adequately thought about their subjects and just start talking. *It's also important for executives to communicate consistently* over a long period of time. Anyone who says one thing today and another tomorrow – whatever suits them – will sooner or later damage their authority.

- **Context**, finally, means the answer to the question: Where do we stand right now? Particularly in large companies, it's often assumed that everyone always knows what's going on. Then, when someone says, "I've thought about it again …", everybody else will wonder: Thought about what? It's better to create the context first. For example: "I've thought about the question of how to finance our project 'Intrepid'."

The 5C principle is universal and applicable regardless of the language in which you communicate. However, languages have their peculiarities, and if you want to communicate easily and understandably in a particular language, then it's worth looking into these specifics. The rudiments of English, for example, the business language No. 1, are easy to learn. However, English is one of the languages with the most extensive vocabulary. For almost everything, there are many alternative expressions. Educated native speakers are therefore sometimes misunderstood by non-native speakers.

A phrase like "This sanction does not avail to mitigate our plight" can already be a challenge for people with good English skills. "This activity won't make our difficult situation any better" means the same, only in a less pompous language. There is no "high English" pronunciation that would be analogous to high German, but the English language has many local dialects. I once met a manager who had a distinct Scottish accent and whose team found it hard to understand him. He could have leaned a bit more towards "BBC pronunciation". In comparison, French is a language with a very manageable vocabulary. On the other hand, it is an old scholarly language, close to Latin. That fact comes with the danger of expressing yourself very abstractly and not graphically enough while speaking French.

When it comes to the pitfalls of the German language, Mark Twain said it all in his satire "The Awful German Language", written in 1880. Mark Twain noticed, for example, that in German, the verb is usually found at the very end – and therefore you have to wait a long time before you can get the meaning of a sentence:

> In a German newspaper they put their verb away over on the next page; and I have heard that sometimes after stringing along the exciting preliminaries and parentheses for a column or two, they get in a hurry and have to go to press without getting to the verb at all. Of course, then, the reader is left in a very exhausted and ignorant state.

Whether it's caused by the verb or not: I think we Germans sometimes need a pretty long start before we get to the essential point. But we can work on that. By the way, the best way to greatly improve your skills in any given language is as simple as it is effective: Read as many books by good authors as possible! You will acquire language skills automatically by reading the books of the masters of any language. At the same time you'll expand your mental horizon – and will also entertain others well.

Communicating digital change – the new challenge?

Simply portraying complex issues has always been an art: How does a scientist in a pharmaceutical company explain a new substance in a way that the layman will understand, too? What arguments does a salesman at a plant manufacturer use to tell a brewery that their old bottling plant still works but that nevertheless they would greatly benefit from a new one? How does the managing director of a consumer goods manufacturer inform shareholders of a persistent problem with the supply chain? Due to digitization, there's now the added problem that even the greatest experts' expert knowledge is outdated within a very short time. Even the gurus and cracks of the digital age have to make sure that they keep pace with it. It is only then that they start thinking about what they want to implement in their own company – and how to communicate it to everybody. I have an appointment with Jörg Hellwig about the particular challenge of communicating digital change. He is CDO of the chemicals group Lanxess, which emerged from sections of Bayer AG in 2004.

We meet in Jörg's office in Cologne; it spontaneously evokes the associations "vision" and "reduction to the essentials" in me. For me, Jörg is also a particularly interesting conversation partner because his career is very atypical for a chief digitizer in a chemical corporation: He is neither a scientist nor an engineer or computer scientist; instead his training started in the production facilities of Bayer when he was 16. He literally worked his way up from the workshop. Today Jörg considers it a great advantage that he went through almost all areas of the company over a period of several decades: production, supply chain, marketing, sales, purchasing, human resources – and that's not all. Precisely because he knows many of the company's processes, he can assess the possibilities of digitization particularly well. Added to this is his ability to look outside the box. Jörg worked for a long time in the United States as well as in India. "I know the world pretty well," he says.

First of all I'm interested in learning what exactly, in Jörg's view, are the opportunities digitization provides. Particularly in the chemical industry. "We open ourselves to new technologies we haven't invented ourselves but that we combine with the enormous knowledge we have about chemistry," Jörg explains. "The same applies to other established industries that have their roots in engineering, for example. In this combination, 1 + 1 is not 2 but rather 5 or 10 or 20. That's what we're seeing right now, and that makes my job so incredibly exciting. In addition, as a CDO, I can do something that has always been my principle: looking for people who are much better than me. Otherwise it won't get us anywhere. I'm not a techie, and in many things I was an idiot at first. I had to look at things and learn a bit."

Perhaps that helps in later being able to explain how things are related to each other and to communicate the intended change?

"That brings us to digitization as such," Jörg says. "There's something very awkward about it: The goal is unknown!" A fundamental difference to traditional change management. "Exactly. We don't know what exactly it means to want to digitize ourselves. We also don't know if we'll be more digital in a year from now. We are starting something new without being able to really say where it will lead. We neither know what it will cost nor whether there will ever be a return on the millions of dollars we've just spent on it. Oddly enough, we only know one thing for sure: If we don't digitize, we'll have more problems than if we digitize."

This unprecedented situation naturally has consequences for the employees. Who really expects that even the top executives don't know exactly where the journey will end? "Absolutely. Specially in a conservative and solid industry like ours. It's all very challenging. You first need a visionary CEO who says, 'I want digitization now. And for a CDO, I'll get an insider who probably thinks like me. Then we'll just start.' That's what happend in our company, and it scared off many people. There was irritation and many fears. Questions like: 'What does digitization mean anyway?' If I don't understand technology, it scares me at first. But then the first people said relatively quickly, 'That's cool; I want to be part of it!' Some of them are people I brought with me from my old job."

One exciting thing about digitization – not the only one, by far – is that we're not able to define goals one hundred per cent. On the other hand, Jörg has a vision. He may not say so explicitly, but that's how I perceive it. How does Jörg succeed in inspiring employees for this vision? Especially people, for example, in production or administration? After all, it's sometimes about extremely complex things. How can I get people excited about issues that are not fully comprehended?

"Clear, simple communication!" Jörg says promptly. "That means we focus on the effectiveness of communication. We keep asking ourselves: Which stories, which examples do all employees understand – from warehouse workers to lab technicians? What can they really relate to? Stories that act as eye openers are a lot more important than comprehensive details: 'Oh, it has something to do with me!' We've been taking that storytelling approach from the start. And what's important, too: Right from the start, we ensured that we had a unique image we could use to communicate the digitization initiative. Recognition is important because there are many initiatives within the corporation. Whether film, newspaper for employees or intranet – we want everyone to immediately understand: 'This is digital'. But that alone is not enough because we can't spread digitization out of a tower."

What does the alternative look like? "We also have to go into production, for example. At least two-thirds of Lanxess employees work in production or close to production. That's still our backbone; it adds value. So what did we do specifically? We bought a few barrels, put a computer unit on top and a screen on top of that. With that, we started the production and showed people some things that are possible with iPhones, QR codes, and so on. We adapted our demonstrations to the different shifts, that is, we didn't do demonstrations Mondays to Fridays from eight to five but according to the shift rhythm; sometimes we even stayed there for 24 hours. We first coordinated with production regarding the best spot where to set things up and how to reach people when they had some spare time. It really added momentum and we were able to get most of the people involved."

What other approaches did they have? "We started a staff blog relatively early," Jörg says. "Many companies do that, but in our corporation it was something that was totally new. There were those at management level who said, 'We want to read everything you write first before you release it.' But that would have been censorship and wouldn't have served the purpose of such a blog. These were just concerns because we had never done such a thing before. We did it anyway, and now it works very well. At the beginning everything was a bit bumpy, but now it really is daily communication and even collaboration! People we would never have reached in any other way – or who we never expected to be interested – are getting involved in digital issues. You just never know the kind of 'other' lives people who work for you have. Somebody might have VR equipment in their basement or develop games in their spare time. We were able to mobilize these people, and they contribute a lot. By the way, it was quite something to learn that we don't just have to let a few board members and business unit leaders play with this issue, but 16,000 people in the company. We want to make 16,000 people more digital!"

I'm also interested in other examples of how Jörg's team reaches out to the company's employees. "'Digital Morning' is another format we use," Jörg says. "Once a month, we invite someone from the outside to talk about any subject related to digitization. We already had people from Amazon and Google here, but also Thomas Lilge from the Humboldt University in Berlin, who specifically talked about gaming. Before the lecture, some people inquired what good that was supposed to be. After the lecture and the subsequent discussion, many people realized that gaming is one of the most successful new tools for further education. 'Serious games' and 'game-based learning' get people a lot more involved than just studying some stupid PowerPoint presentation. We then went so far as to go to gamescom with people. Even a board member joined us. That was when most of them started to understand what's going on in that scene. Our idea was also that someone who's walking around the trade fair halls in a Darth Vader costume today might be the purchasing manager of our largest client tomorrow. We're in an industry that still sends order confirmations by fax and where many people are still using the phone a lot. We want people to say themselves, 'No, we don't want that anymore', and that's what's happening now."

My conversation with Jörg once again clearly illustrated what good communication is all about. It's important to go to people instead of spreading messages from the top. And not only to go to them but also to get them involved and to start a dialogue with them. And, particularly – but not only – where digitization is concerned, the insight that everyone of us is still learning is important. Those who still consider themselves to be omniscient are not credible. Even the CEO of Lanxess, as Jörg mentions, says quite openly that he has to learn something

> It's important to go to people instead of spreading messages from the top. And not only to go to them but also to get them involved and to start a dialogue with them.

new every day because there are more and more new things. Finally, the conversation has also shown that simple and effective communication requires many small approaches instead of one big hit. That's what I believe in, and that's why I want to conclude this chapter with some specific tips and hints.

The art of communicating easily and clearly every day

When it comes to communication, the first thing many people may think of is the big speech at the staff meeting. Or the kick-off meeting where visions are explained and goals are set. Or the circular mail to the whole team. All that is doubtlessly important. Equally important, however, is the sum of many small details in everyday business. Simple and clear communication helps in countless situations and can be practiced daily. It even makes a difference how I word the subject of an email or what words I use to invite employees to a meeting! I have already explained the 5-C principle. It's kind of like a compass for any form of communication. Finally, there are still a few blank spots on the map: Tips and hints that originate from the 5-C principle. At the same time, let me summarize a few points that have already been discussed in various sections of this chapter.

What should you pay particular attention to when communicating in your daily job?

- Whenever you communicate, **emotions** are always part of the game. Appreciation towards employees is often shown by the fact that you don't just transmit the bare facts but also emotions. The military tone should really be confined to the military today. Those who, instead of saying "Meeting tomorrow, 9:00 a. m.", word their message this way: "I'm looking forward to meeting you tomorrow at 9:00 a. m. and can't wait to hear your ideas", which doesn't only allow for emotions but also expresses appreciation. In addition, courtesy may be old-fashioned but it isn't outdated! Appreciation also means never communicating from the top down but always at eye level. Reach out to people whenever you can!

- **Stories and examples** are essential. Images and stories are the language of our subconscious. That's also why we dream stories and not facts at night. Use small stories and examples wherever possible. Also describe what you experienced, what you noticed in the company or outside of it. Find **imagery and metaphors** to explain difficult facts. Why is it that anyone understands the term "computer virus" so much faster and better than the term "malware"? Because it's imagery!

- Don't hide behind incomprehensible **technical words** and avoid exotic and redundant **abbreviations**. There are industry-specific technical terms that every employee in production knows. That's not what I'm talking about. Even a certain business jargon – with terms such as corporate, benchmark or unit – is okay as long as your listeners are executives, too. The same applies to common abbreviations such as CEO or ROI. It will be difficult if many of your listeners don't really understand you because they don't know your technical terms or abbreviations. You should explore the boundaries from case to case. It's important that you're aware of that problem!

- Write short and concise **emails** and use an informative **subject line**. Instead of using an outdated subject line when responding to an old email – as some people do – spend most of the time thinking about the subject line. It should contain the message in the shortest form possible. So don't write "Our project" but rather, for instance, "€ 20 000 required for Project Blue Sky by Friday". At FocusFirst, we also put certain tags in square brackets in front of the text. For example, [Action required], [Approval required] or [Question]. This way the recipient knows right away what response this email requires.

- When giving **presentations**, pay attention to this rule: First word the message to the point, then present the details. Generally, don't overload your slides with information and refrain from any slides you don't need. Also focus on images and stories, not just facts, when giving your presentation. Books, videos and blogs with titles such as "Presenting the Way Steve Jobs Does It" are popular for a reason. You can learn a lot from the masters of presentation. The same applies to **lectures**. For example, the TED Talks are very inspiring. TED chief Chris Anderson has also written an instructive book about it (*TED Talks: The Official TED Guide to Public Speaking*).

- Here's another tip for advanced speakers: Apply **framing**. Frames are "conceptual frames of interpretation". Some scientists claim that framing unconsciously determines how a message is received. Example: When saying "We've *enlisted* 10 per cent of new customers" or "We've *won over* 10 per cent of new customers", you're using two different frames for the same factual statement: either the frame "battle" or "war" or the frame "good fortune" or "success" . The identical fact is subconsciously perceived differently. There are exciting books and online sources available on the subject of framing.

This brings us nearly to the end of this book – but only nearly. Chapter 1 dealt with the inner desire to want to do something great and meaningful, and the question of what you need for epic stuff. In Chapter 2, we examined limits and limiting factors in our minds and how to overcome them. You learned in Chapter 3 why focus is so important because you can't do everything at the same time, but you can do the right things. Once you're inspired and focused, you need the right culture for epic stuff, and that's what Chapter 4 is all about. In Chapter 5, you saw that you can never do great things alone, but it doesn't matter because there are always thousands of others who can help you if you only go out and get them. Chapter 6 was about the emotionally touching narrative that really motivates everyone in the team. How important it is to deliver in the end, and how you can do that – this is what you learned from Chapter 7. In this chapter, it's all about how you communicate easily and purposefully every day. What now? Now you have almost all the building blocks you need for epic stuff. And perhaps you've already made other people hot for the big goal. Very well. Then you can now take responsibility for everything! That's what the final chapter is all about.

Chapter 9

Do It, or Else Nobody Will: Assuming Responsibility

Anil let his Panamera coast along the harbour front at a walking pace. To his left, the Elbe River sparkled in the evening sun. A container ship of the Mærsk Line, which was on its way to the Port of Hamburg, cast its shadow close to the banks of the Elbe. Anil was looking for one of the coveted vacant parking spaces on the right-hand curb of the road. He spotted the company car of Thomas, his co-CEO, a silver-coloured S-class Mercedes, in the long line of parked cars. Anil wasn't happy about the fact that Thomas was already here, more than fifteen minutes early. After all, meeting for dinner at the restaurant "Skipper House" had been his idea. He intended it to lead to a clarifying talk about the two managing directors' respective areas of responsibilities. But Thomas didn't know that yet. Anil had invited Thomas to dinner, and the second CEO had accepted his invitation. Anil spotted a vacant parking spot some distance away, right next to the steps that led to the "Skipper House." "Well, at least that's going according to plan," he thought and stepped on the gas. Right before reaching the narrow parking spot, he activated the parking assistant at the push of a button and let the Porsche park itself.

After Anil had locked the car and walked up the steps to the restaurant, he smiled: Even though the fact that Thomas had shown up first was unpleasant for him, it was typical of their business association. In the company, it was also Thomas who seemed to have been around forever. Anil was already the third CEO of the large manufacturer of medical technology in the last 10 years. The owners expected him to finally get the digitization of the company on the road, something his two predecessors had not managed to accomplish. Thomas, on the other hand, had been co-CEO for more than 25 years and, according to the organizational chart, he was responsible for "finances and organization". He had seen others like Anil coming and going, but he himself had always remained Number Two: a meticulous and diligent man who was good with numbers, dates, and facts. He made his appearance once a year at the presentation of the annual balance sheet and the subsequent press conference. During the rest of the year he stayed in the background.

Thomas was sitting at one of the tables by the window, wearing a light gray suit, a white shirt and a red-and-white striped tie and reading the printed edition of the FT. He had already ordered a large bottle of mineral water and two glasses. His manners were impeccable. Anil was also still wearing his work outfit, which, however, consisted of light-coloured jeans, a summer jacket and a linen shirt without a tie. Thomas put the newspaper down as soon as Anil approached the table and got up to say hello to his colleague. Every time they met, the two CEOs needed a moment to tune into each other. Anil was vivacious; he liked to laugh and always had an exciting story to tell. Thomas was always polite, but he rarely smiled and hardly ever laughed. For Anil, the man with the short gray hair was someone he'd buy the proverbial used car from without hesitating. You could count on Thomas' accuracy as well as on his honesty.

As etiquette required, Anil waited until after dessert before addressing the reason for this meeting. "I've been in the company for almost a year now; I feel right at home there and really enjoy working with you, too," Anil said to Thomas. "I value your knowledge and experience, and I know I can rely on you one hundred per cent." Thomas listened attentively without showing any emotions. "However, there's one point I'd like to clarify with you," Anil continued. "I've noticed that many of the employees don't know what exactly you're responsible for and what not. Sure, 'finances' is obvious, and I'll stay out of it. For me, you are the epitome of the honourable Hanseatic merchant and the perfect cast for the financial sector. But what does 'organization' include? This term is not common, and I've never seen it used in any other large company. No matter who came up with this term at some point: It's my impression that the employees mainly see 'organization' as something that they'd rather discuss with you than with me. And honestly, Thomas: If something is clearly within my area of responsibility, then I want you to send the people to me."

Anil paused. He had summed up the basics without beating around the bush, just as he had planned to do. Thomas was silent for thirty seconds. Anil was prepared for a difficult discussion. Then Thomas said in his normal soft, sober tone of voice, "I've never thought about that. But now that you say it, I think your observation is totally correct. I think, particularly the older employees come to me because they've known me for so long. But you're absolutely right: That's not correct. I won't just send the people to you from now on. But I'll also communicate clearly once again what I'm responsible for and what not. I hope that's been clarified by now." Anil looked at Thomas and shrugged. "It isn't?" Thomas asked. "Well, then let's talk about it. In addition to finances, I've always taken care of the trivial things so that the first CEO won't be bothered with them. I'm ultimately responsible for making the elevators work and for the lights in the garage. That's all the term 'organization' we use in our company covers."

When everybody wants to be part of it but nobody accepts responsibility

Many people who want to make a difference in large corporations can relate to what Anil addressed here with his co-CEO Thomas (the names, industry and location have been changed for this story, too): Clearly defined responsibilities are the exception rather than the rule. The rule is that responsibilities are not clearly defined and that nobody likes to address them. And the worst case scenario? That is that some people water down their responsibilities on purpose. For some employees in large companies, the motto seems to be, "I like to be part of everything but I can't always do much about something." In plain language: I'm not ready to accept responsibility. Sometimes you have two employees who both want to have the last word. One of them may be higher up in the hierarchy while the other one has long-standing claims and is better networked. That was the situation with Anil and Thomas. Unfortunately, it's not common for one of them to accept responsibility and seek to clarify matters. It's rather the laudable exception for someone to attempt to clarify responsibilities of their own accord.

This kind of clarification may also be unpleasant at first. It requires confronting another individual, and you never know how the other person will react. That's why, in my experience, the two opponents will just leave things the way they are and come to terms with the fact that there will always be trouble. This way, their work may be only 70 per cent effective, and never 100 per cent. But they somehow come to terms with that. Those who want to be part of everything come to terms as well. Although they may know that they won't be able to do their share in the end, they accept that their issues and projects plod along at a level of perhaps 60 or 70 per cent. They'd rather do that than spell out the next time what they really want to do and what they don't feel like doing.

> There is no business without risk.

All this is not a lack of competence or experience, of imagination or creativity, not even of intrinsic motivation or enthusiasm. It's simply a lack of willingness to accept responsibility. Instead, this is about needing to feel secure, minimizing risks and not losing face. But there is no business without risk. All of the great founders and entrepreneurs of the past, who gave their names to many of the corporate giants of today, knew that. Their names were Bosch or Siemens, Ford or Toyota, Merck or Boeing. Today, every child in the world knows the brands that bear their names. All of these founders took great risks. No one opted for the easy way out. All of them suffered setbacks, and all of them, really all of them, accepted responsibility for their actions at all times.

The same is true for the founders and entrepreneurs of Silicon Valley today. They breathe the same spirit as entrepreneurs did 100 or 200 years ago. And even if we don't always like everything the big tech companies do that were start-ups just 15, 20 years ago: Jeff Bezos, Elon Musk and Mark Zuckerberg have accepted full responsibility for what they do. So if you want to do epic stuff, don't act like a state official. Instead think, talk and act like a founder or entrepreneur. Epic stuff doesn't mean: "Play it safe." It means: "No risk, no gain."

> Think, talk and act like a founder or entrepreneur. Epic stuff doesn't mean: "Play it safe." It means: "No risk, no gain."

There's a magic formula for epic stuff in a corporate, a Harry-Potter-like abracadabra. This magic formula consists of only three words, but these three words will change everything. They read: I TAKE RESPONSIBILITY. When a leader says, "I take responsibility," that will provide security for everyone else. So use this formula for yourself and say it aloud. When you take on a new role, take a white piece of paper and write on top in your handwriting, "That's what I'm responsible for". Below that, you list everything you now have assumed responsibility for. You may list what you need for each point in a second column. By filling in this sheet of paper, you are taking responsibility. Then communicate this to your team as well. If they address a point on your list, then say clearly: "That's my responsibility." You'll often feel a boost of energy the very moment you say that. Practice it with little things, too. If someone says, "Somebody has to organize the company party", this is your opportunity to answer, "I'll be responsible for it." And then do it, too.

If you're enthusiastic, you'll also enjoy accepting responsibility

Some plans work out, others don't: My original plan was to fly to Vienna and meet Ludwig Askemper, Managing Director of Mondelez Austria. Our schedules did not let us do that, so one Saturday we sit down to Skype. And it has something to do with responsibility that made us say, "Okay, our Plan A doesn't seem to work for the near future. So let's instead go for Plan B and hold our conversation via Skype, rather than postponing it or even giving up our plan." I certainly didn't want the latter! I'm really happy that Ludwig is taking the time to talk to me at the weekend. Mondelez is a global player and is literally on everyone's lips with brands such as Milka, Oreo, or Cadbury. Ludwig – who incidentally grew up in a large family on a farm, as he tells me – returned to the company as reorganizer in a challenging situation at a time when he actually wanted to withdraw from the corporate world to devote himself to other interests. First of all, I want to know how it came about that he assumed responsibility once again. When a leader is expected to accomplish a turnaround, that task usually is not a walk in the park.

"My former boss called me and asked me to help him," Ludwig says. "Now I always enjoyed working with him and owe him a lot. That's one of the main reasons why it didn't take me long to say: Okay, I'll do it. I'll make it my responsibility – even and particularly in a challenging situation. I had already achieved several turnarounds in other places before. Not as your typical tough troubleshooter but because of the way I deal with teams and unite them behind an idea. In addition, confectionery has a long tradition. Many have fallen in love with it, and for me, too, that was a motive to take responsibility. After all, I knew it was really about the matter per se and not a demonstration of power or emergency management. Otherwise I wouldn't have done it. My experience in sales was what helped me to envision the turnaround. Many leaders aren't really close to sales and therefore know little about the technical aspects. I'm certainly one of the few in such a position who, at the start of their careers, would drive from shop to shop for years and sell products. I knew that would help me."

I really like that story. Curious about details, I want to learn more about three points. My first question is: How exactly does Ludwig assume responsibility? My second question is: Why is that important to him, and what's the reward for him personally? And my third question is: How does he manage to get others to assume responsibility, too? "It's just a wonderful feeling for me to help other people get back on track when things aren't going well. Even more so when the challenge is so great that it becomes a once-in-a-lifetime experience, as it is now here in Vienna. I often imagine meeting the people I work with again years

> It's this anticipatory retrospect – to already picture now how it will be when I've accomplished it.

later, and they'll say, "Do you remember, back when …" It's this anticipation of looking back – to already picture now how it will be when I've accomplished it – that already feels like victory to me." I can relate to that last point particularly well! It's not a coincidence that the anticipation of the future takes up that much space in this book. And what about the responsibility of others?

"To answer that question, I need to reach back a bit. Specially in difficult situations, when we're getting closer to the turnaround, the 20-60-20 rule is time and again confirmed with regard to the people: 20 per cent immediately understand what needs to be done and ca cry out, Hooray! On the other hand, there are 20 per cent who understand it but don't want and sometimes can't do it. They don't care about responsibility for the whole matter but only about their own short-term interests. And then there's that large block of 60 per cent who wait and see what happens. My approach has always been to try to get as many people as possible – and especially the right people – on the side of the first 20 per cent. My ultimate goal is to arouse entrepreneurial enthusiasm. People should just enjoy doing business. If that's the case, then they will also enjoy assuming responsibility. But as I said, there are those people who want to prevent the turnaround. Although that's actually incomprehensible. Yet I don't fight them but rather try to awaken the ambition of those who do want it. It's about being able to say at some point: Wow, that was quite the mountain, but we did it! And not just that: We want to have a great time together and experience exciting moments in a team on our way there. You can make the working hours very exciting for yourself and others, and do it in a way that makes it a pleasure to go to work."

Many people don't necessarily associate enthusiasm and joy with difficult situations or even with a turnaround. I like the fact that, for Ludwig, enthusiasm, especially in difficult situations, is the key to accomplishing the turnaround! That means that the greater my joy, the more I enjoy taking responsibility. "Yet I wouldn't put too much emphasis on the term 'responsibility' and, above all, not constantly talk about it," Ludwig adds thoughtfully. "'Responsibility' was one of the five

> Responsibility is a big word. It shouldn't have that much weight and it shouldn't be a burden.

principles of a company I was in for a long time – and that's way too much for my liking. 'Responsibility' is a big word. It shouldn't have that much weight and it shouldn't be a burden. Of course I assume responsibility, and of course I have to get things out of the way. But after that, it's much nicer to think of the perspective, the excitement behind it, the journey that awaits you. As soon as enthusiasm comes into play, the seriousness that often accompanies the word 'responsibility' is gone." So it's better not to talk about "responsibility" all the time but to willingly take responsibility – and then focus on working on that one big goal with enthusiasm and joy. I consider that a very valuable message at this point.

How intrapreneurs think and act in the company

People who take the responsibility for big goals in a corporate are also called 'intrapreneurs', which is a very appropriate term for them. They have the mentality of an internal entrepreneur, an entrepreneur within the company. They do their jobs with enthusiasm and joy – even when the going gets tough. Just as Ludwig Askemper described it in our conversation. When others already start whining, intrapreneurs keep focusing on the big goal and ensure that their spirits remain positive. They think big and are convinced that things will work out. They are doers, have a pronounced *can-do* mentality and get actively involved when the situation demands it, as Daniel Szabo described it so wonderfully in our conversation. Intrapreneurs are fast and proactive. They can handle risks. Instead of dealing with risks and thinking of failing, however, they prefer to deal with the opportunities they get. "Responsibility" is often a big word and sometimes even a hollow one. In that aspect, I quite agree with Ludwig Askemper. To me, people who assume responsibility in a corporate are intrapreneurs as I've just described them. That has a lot more to do with rolled-up sleeves than with framed guidelines.

The attitude of an entrepreneur when dealing with risks, obstacles and hurdles may be precisely expressed with one phrase: "Love it, change it or leave it." If I bear the responsibility and something doesn't work out the way I expected, then I first ask myself: Is it really that bad? Will it hurt me or us? It might just be okay and not worth thinking about. In that case: If there's something positive in all this, what could that be? Maybe then I'll discover that everything is fine the way it is. That's "love it". There is this legend about the inventor of credit cards, Frank McNamara, who, while having lunch at a restaurant in New York in 1950, realized that he had forgotten his wallet. So he paid with his business card – his "good reputation" – and later returned to pay his bill in cash. His attitude shows what a great entrepreneur he was: It must have embarrassed McNamara to have forgotten his wallet – but instead of getting annoyed, he immediately found a solution to the problem. And that solution led to his brilliant business idea! In the end, forgetting his wallet even had something positive.

> The attitude of an entrepreneur when dealing with risks, obstacles and hurdles may be precisely expressed with one phrase: "Love it, change it or leave it."

"Change it" means: Okay, it can't go on like that; something is blocking our way – some rocks that are just too big. Since I'm responsible for that, I must also make sure they're cleared away. It's not my workers who are responsible, it's nobody else but me. Of course it's not always necessary to do everything yourself. But I myself stay on it and don't give up until the problem is solved. Joachim Jäckle, Henkel's former CIO, described that kind of situation impressively in our conversation: During a cyber attack, he sat with his employees in the crisis room for days and nights at a stretch. Not because he was able to do anything about it on the technical level – only the computer experts could do that – but because he had assumed the responsibility for the problem being solved as quickly as possible.

Should the obstacles be too high despite all efforts, for an intrapreneur, responsibility means stepping on the brakes. That's what "leave it" means. This includes inner greatness and usually courage, too. Even if there are a dozen or more other people who have screwed up things, an intrapreneur will say, "I'll take responsibility for that." Fortunately, the start-up culture has changed many things for the better. Failure is part of life and may occur in companies, too. What I learn from setbacks is what counts.

After all, intrapreneurs are also characterized by being able to motivate others to assume responsibility. Nobody can do epic stuff on their own. The team may also take responsibility. Ultimately, it's up to the individual to decide. As a leader, I can't make that decision for anyone else. I can, however, create a sense of belonging and inspire people. By having a positive mind and by arousing enthusiasm, I make it easier for people to assume responsibility. I'm also responsible for ensuring that my team has everything it needs right from the start and won't be faced with any avoidable obstacles at any point. Chapter 7 described this in detail. However, as soon as all requirements are met, I can expect binding commitments from the members of my team, too.

> Nobody can do epic stuff on their own. The team may also take responsibility.

Anyone who can see the big picture, will ask themselves: Am I the right person for the job?

At the Henkel headquarters in Dusseldorf I meet the CDO, Dr. Rahmyn Kress. He was born in Germany, spent the first 14 years of his life there, and has been living in London ever since. I ask Rahmyn right away how it came about that he switched to Henkel as CDO and was responsible for digitization. Before he joined the traditional consumer goods company, his career had been diverse as well as exciting: The economist started as a banker, which is an obvious profession to get into in London, but in the long run it wasn't his cup of tea. "It was either a coincidence or my destiny" that he ended up first in the film industry and later in the music industry, Rahmyn says with a wink. At MCA and Universal Music he had already shouldered a lot of responsibility at a very young age and could "always decide which role I was to play in small teams and create my own job", he recalls. In 2010, he left the music industry to establish a technology company in France. It was eventually bought by Accenture and became one of the first pillars of today's Accenture Digital. Rahmyn initially joined Accenture and managed Accenture Ventures to bring start-ups and corporations together, among other things. Which almost brings us to Henkel. But how exactly did that happen? And what motivated Rahmyn to assume responsibility as CDO?

"I was managing Accenture Ventures when a partner said to me, 'I have a major client who wants to understand the issue of start-ups. Can you help me? I'm supposed to bring the management team in Berlin together with a few start-ups and founders for one day.' Together with a few friends from the Axel Springer Accelerator – APX today – I presented a kind of general introduction to start-ups for Henkel and showed what they mean for corporations. Then one of Henkel's board members approached me and asked, 'We're looking for a CDO; do you know anyone? Or could you help us and tell us what to look for?' My first reaction was, 'What do you think you need a CDO for? This is just a fad; everybody wants a CDO now. But what should that person do for you?' So we started talking about that subject right away. I said, 'I can give you some guidelines, but it's not for me.' Later, we had a lot of discussions in the larger circle, and in the end they asked me, 'Wouldn't you be interested in doing it after all?' And yes, at that point and after the rounds of discussion that we had been having until then, I actually was interested."

At first, Rahmyn had not only asked why Henkel needed a CDO but also contributed his own ideas and experiences to the discussion. "I said if Henkel wants to hire a CDO, then this and this should be the task areas and reporting lines," he recalls. "Henkel then made me that offer, and because I thought it would be a great opportunity to help an organization with such a history to continue to play an important role in the future, I became CDO in June 2017. Henkel is now 142 years old; it was founded by an entrepreneur and has many incredibly positive values. In addition, I had been in the same boat in the music industry when it missed the digital disruption. Now I can almost say: I repent and will do a better job this time. So in the end I was happy to accept that job. And I felt and still feel really very, very humble, considering the enormous heritage of this company. With such a story, you have to be respectful and can't just say, 'That's all nonsense; we'll change it.' At the same time, you really want to make a difference. It's a very delicate issue and quite a challenge."

How does Rahmyn now see the role of the CDO, since he can no longer dismiss it as a fad because he has played it himself? "Today I think, yes, a chief digital officer can be useful, but it depends on the organization and on how long he stays on," Rahmyn says. "In my view, the CDO always comes with an expiration date. I joined Henkel in the summer of 2017. Now it's the summer of 2019, and in October I will hand my digital transformation tasks over to my successor. A good CDO should be aware of the fact that he's a pioneer and a catalyst, no more and no less. If he has made himself redundant, he has achieved his goal. When I started here, I said that I wanted to make the transformation within the next two years. Now everyone out there suddenly thinks we'll permanently be seeing transformation in the future, but I disagree. We will have permanent innovation, but the transformation itself – other processes, a new culture, the integration of all pilot projects into the core business, and so on – is a unique event. And I really believe that corporations can do that very well. They've been doing it for more than 200 years."

The way Rahmyn describes his task sounds like he's already on the home stretch after his two years with Henkel. "That's true. I'm very proud of what has been achieved, and it's not all on my account. You're always measured by your results. If you take on this job and realize after a year that you can't get the organization transformed, that doesn't mean you're no good. You may just be the wrong person for this job in this environment. Then you should be honest enough and look for someone else who will replace you and give them better results than you can." Not everyone will assume so much responsibility for the big picture. "No, only a few do that. It helps if we see ourselves as being some kind of drug: Even the best drug won't work for some patients. Not because the drug is bad, but because these patients need some other kind of medicine. Only if you, as CDO, realize that you really are the catalyst of change, you're the right person for the job. That's what happened to me in the last two years. Everyone here has been doing a great job. Therefore the right time for me to change jobs will come soon. Henkel will hire a new Chief Digital and Information Officer, who will then secure the scaling and continue to support the company by using the current momentum."

Let's talk a bit about Henkel X. It's kind of the centrepiece of what Rahmyn has initiated at Henkel. "I founded Henkel X in February 2018," he explains. "I wanted the corporation to do it all on its own, which has shown to be successful when it comes to start-ups and young, fast-growing companies. And to do it without entering the world of start-ups and incubators, which I don't consider value-adding. I think that it may even be potentially harmful. It's best for a corporation with all its talents and competencies, financial resources, distribution channels, customers, and so on, to bring the start-up methods into the company. For that purpose we first looked for excellent mentors. The approximately 200 mentors Henkel X has today come from the venture capital scene and entrepreneurship. You find some real game changers of the digital economy among them. When we got the mentors together, we wanted to network in our industry across Europe, and we launched the Industry Partnership Program, which today brings many German DAX corporations and similarly sized companies from France, Spain, Italy, and other countries together."

What is at issue? "We'll think about 'Retail 2030', for example, and tell ourselves that we don't want to leave the visions up to Amazon. When Henkel, Nestlé, three large retail chains and two other consumer goods companies sit around the table, exchanging ideas and even getting entrepreneurs to join them as mentors, this may result in an idea that makes us think, 'Let's try that.' By that I mean: We'll try it together; we'll either fail or suceed together. The success Henkel X enjoys is groundbreaking. Our relationships with other companies are getting better and better, we can be out on the market extremely fast, and more and more entrepreneurs want to join us. We can finance these entrepreneurs, support them and let them try out our products. Henkel X has already grown enormously. We believe in Europe and want to become the Central European platform for open innovation."

Many companies have people who would like to do something similar to what Rahmyn does. But they don't even start. They are like people who don't want to learn to ride a bicycle because they're afraid they might fall off. Or they don't want to be beginners because others might laugh at them. But everyone has to start somewhere. What advice does Rahmyn have for those who can't muster the courage to assume the responsibility for big goals and just start? "First of all, there are no patent recipes that work for everyone," Rahmyn says. "With BMW, I'd already have to do a lot of things differently from

> Try things, make the results quantifiable, and if they're not immediately good, ask yourself why they're not good.

here. So when people say they don't want to join Henkel X but would rather do their own thing, I say, great! We don't see them as competitors. Not everything someone touches will turn into gold right away. Nevertheless, I think 'fail fast' is utter nonsense. It's not about failure. So don't focus on it. Try things, make the results quantifiable, and if they're not good right away, ask yourself why they're not good. The next point: inspiration is important, but inspiration alone is boasting. You must achieve quantifiable results. You need tools; you need mentors; you need good communication. What you don't need are 50,000 'entrepreneurs in the company'. That, too, is utter nonsense. Be proud of your people in production and use their knowledge because their knowledge is tremendous. Pay attention to your messages and never promise too much. If you say your door is always open and anyone can come in to see you, then you must mean it. Otherwise, don't say that sort of thing!" So you could also summarize it in one sentence: Take full responsibility for your words and deeds!

Why you have less to lose than you may think

I worked for a long time in a corporate myself and was responsible for global projects. And today, with FocusFirst, I get to know many large companies from the inside. I've often caught myself shaking my head and walking down a corridor, wondering: What are so many people here afraid of? What makes them so discouraged and lets them hesitate that long before assuming responsibility? I don't mean that in a condescending way, but I really do ask myself that question. One answer may be that too many people envision all kinds of scenarios, thinking about what could go wrong and what consequences that would have. I can only agree with Rahmyn Kress when he says that focusing on failure is totally wrong. Once you have a working system of performance indicators and review your results on a regular basis, you don't have to worry about potential failure. *Where focus goes, energy flows.* So keep your focus on the positive target image!

I often get the impression that for many people, their greatest fear is personal failure. They think, "If this is going to be an epic fail instead of epic stuff, that'll be it for me and I'll lose my job!" That concern may be the real reason why they water down their responsibilities or never commit themselves. But are such fears justified at all? More than 99.9 per cent of the things we're afraid of will never happen. And we can take care of the few things that do

> More than 99.9 per cent of the things we're afraid of will never happen.

go wrong when they occur. So ask yourself: What could really happen to me? In many Western European countries it is easier to get a divorce than to let go of an employee. But even in other parts of the world you don't have to expect to be fired at any time. Based on my experience, a lot has to happen in the corporate world before somebody is actually fired. And many of those who have a good lawyer will still get a settlement they can live off for several years.

To some people, it sounds a bit fantastic when I say that as soon as you concentrate fully on your future success every day, you will almost certainly have that success. You can try the methods and advice provided in this book and see if they work for you. However, trying things out doesn't mean doing things halfheartedly. Taking full responsibility is part of the package. If you want to fly a plane, you can't say: I'll fly a bit, and when I'm 18,000 ft up in the air, I'll think about whether I want to fly any further. And while balancing on a tightrope, you can't say, I'll go halfway down the rope and see if I want to go any further. Either you do it or you don't do it. You may think about whether you want to continue flying or balancing on a rope in the future only after you have completed it.

Your only concern should be your focus. Interestingly enough, most people overlook the greatest risk of epic stuff, namely that of losing focus. You can't assume the responsibility for 1000 things at the same time. So be courageous while making sure you don't turn into a mindless responsibility-assumption-machine. Motto:

> Interestingly enough, most people overlook the greatest risk of epic stuff, namely that of losing focus.

I'm head of epic stuff and also president of the local golf club and treasurer of the tennis club, head of the PTA at my daughter's school, chairman of the art museum support association, member of the supervisory board of a hospital association, and so on. Your responsibility must be wherever you want to achieve big goals. In the end, that doesn't have much to do with the issue of responsibility but rather concerns the topic of focus. If your focus remains on a clear goal, then it may even be important to take responsibility beyond the narrow boundaries of your formal area of responsibility. One who exemplifies this is Dirk Ramhorst, CIO and CDO at Wacker Chemie.

Taking matters into your own hands – and letting others benefit from them

I meet Dirk Ramhorst at the corporate headquarters of Wacker Chemie in Munich. As the native Westphalian tells me right away, I'm actually only meeting one of his "two personalities": the businessman. The other personality is the sailor and chief of the Kieler Woche sailing regatta. A man who loves the northern light and for whom water seems to be something he just needs in his life. Dirk, who describes himself as a real "doer", is in charge of organizing one of the world's largest sailing regattas, an event that has a long tradition. Shortly before our meeting, the 138th year of the regatta was celebrated during the 125th Kieler Woche.

Dirk calls the intrinsic motivation he and 450 other volunteers show every year his "fountain of youth". Dirk also has two academic degrees: He studied both software engineering and business administration. Knowing both worlds – IT and business – very well has shaped him throughout his professional life, he says. He says what he's doing in the corporate world in the wake of digitization – figuratively speaking – is more surfing than sailing. When working for BASF, Dirk was the first CDO in a DAX corporation. By now he has been with the smaller Wacker Chemie with its approximately 15,000 employees for three years. At first he was CIO, later he also became CDO.

To me, digitization seems to be a mammoth task for a rather conservative company like Wacker Chemie. So we will talk about how to achieve big goals in such an environment and what it means to take responsibility for them. "A lot of commitment and dedication is always necessary for big goals. But it's important not to stay in one's microcosm," Dirk says with conviction. "I can only change the microcosm if I adapt the bigger picture. That means I don't only handle the changes in the IT section here but also a lot of other things. I just had a conversation about New Work. I also have to deal with the demographic challenge and think about how we can recruit new employees for Wacker. In the next few years I will lose almost half of my employees due to retirement. So I keep talking to people, which isn't that easy as there is a lot of competition right here in Munich. However, I can't afford to say that I am responsible for IT here and that others should look for new people. Yes, I have an area of responsibility, and that includes what I can influence directly. But I think on a larger scale beyond that area. Ultimately because it's in my own interest, so that I can actually change what I want to change."

> Yes, I have an area of responsibility, and that includes what I can influence directly. But I think on a larger scale beyond that area.

Are there any other examples of this expansion of his area of responsibility? "Yes, certainly. At Wacker, for example, there is a so-called executive development programme for junior executives. They pass through several departments in-house, to get to know different methods and ways of working on the one hand, and to grow into their management role on the other hand. I periodically arrange entire event days for our new hires. For example, one day focuses exclusively on agility. On that day we do exercises together to experience agility, practice design thinking and similar things. But we also visit companies here in Munich; we talk with lecturers and students at the UnternehmerTUM event, and we visit start-ups. Those are the themes I bring closer to the people. And there might be someone from my own area, i. e. from IT, among them. The others come from all kinds of different business areas and regions. Everyone senses that something is going on. By doing that, I live up to my role of being the disrupter and also a catalyst who takes his environment to a different energy level. You could say that I 'carry others along'. Your own experience is always the decisive factor. I get things moving and let others experience that movement."

Because of the movement and the new experience the organization will change step by step. And then someone must assume the responsibility for that. It doesn't matter if it falls into one's own area of responsibility or if it goes a little further. I also detect a lot of autonomy, combined with the endeavour to encourage others and also to lead them in that direction, in Dirk's statements. "The part about the autonomy is right," Dirk agrees. "The freedom I had when I switched from BASF to Wacker even intensified my sense of that. If you had asked me before whether I needed a sabbatical, I would've said, 'Nope, why do you ask?' But being out of the corporate world for a couple of months worked very well for me. During those months I accompanied people from medium-sized companies on their trips to Silicon Valley. These were mostly family businesses of the 'hidden champion' type. I was in California with the founders or directors, sometimes with the 'next gen', i.e. their kids. The question was always: 'What are they doing in Silicon Valley that makes all these start-ups so successful – and how are we doing things compared to them?' One summary was often that the position of the German medium-sized companies isn't all that bad after all. Many entrepreneurs from here remembered their own roots in Silicon Valley, i.e. what led to the founding of their companies, namely entrepreneurial thinking. That's the core of their success. All of these family businesses that are huge now – Wacker is one of them – just have to think and act more like entrepreneurs. That means, at the place where the action is and not according to the motto: 'Let my boss decide that.' You don't always need that 100 per cent solution. That's what entrepreneurs do. 'Agility' is actually very old; we only need to remember our original entrepreneurial virtues and can use them to empower ourselves."

Does Silicon Valley still serve as a role model for Dirk in his current role? "Well, figuratively speaking, I often go to Silicon Valley," Dirk confirms. "Not because I get direct impulses for my industry there. But because I bring back a lot of mindset for my work environment here at Wacker as well as for my role at the Kieler Woche from Silicon Valley. And then I take it into my hands to pass it on." So don't just watch but also do it yourself! "Exactly. Everyone has absorbed this mindset, and today they no longer see so many risks, but rather opportunities, when looking at Silicon Valley. After that, we decided to spread it much wider in the company. That's how the idea for the Silicon Valley Challenge was born."

What's that about? "An 18-member group made up of three teams of six members each was to live in Silicon Valley for four weeks to develop ideas. All of our nearly 15,000 employees could apply for it. But not in the form of an application. Instead, we said, 'Just send us something; get creative!' Most of them sent us either videos or something haptic they had put together themselves. We had about 370 applicants, among whom we selected the 18 successful candidates. The participants came from China, Korea, Singapore, Germany, Sweden, Brazil, the U. S., and Thailand. Ten women and eight men. The oldest individual was in his mid-forties, the others were younger than that. Teams of three shared an Airbnb with just one bathroom in Silicon Valley and worked in a co-working space provided by WeWork. They visited start-ups but also shared some unusual activities, such as a rally through San Francisco to study graffiti and even make graffiti themselves. In those four weeks, the teams evaluated hundreds of ideas and then completed one – in one case even two – ideas in four sprints."

How thrilling! What happened after that? "In the end, they went from Silicon Valley directly back to Munich to really pitch the ideas. The board selected three out of four topics as being worth promoting. These three topics are extremely relevant and are still being implemented. I was in Silicon Valley when it started, and a second time right in the middle of the project. Actually, I was just kind of like the tour guide because of my affinity for the region. Then sparks started to fly, and that turned into a controlled wildfire." What a great story! This is exactly what I mean by "assuming responsibility": You have an affinity for a topic, you see a wonderful opportunity – and then you go, take the matter into your own hands, organize something, get the right people together, and in the end you take care of the sustainable implementation. The headline of this chapter – "Do It, or Else Nobody Will" – could also be Dirk Ramhorst's motto.

You alone are responsible for yourself and your actions – anywhere and everywhere

We're all not business robots but humans. People with diverse interests, relationships and responsibilities. Your mindset may look a bit different in business than it does in your personal life, but you're always one person, that one, whole person. You may not be able to accomplish everything in life because your energy and attention are limited. But you can almost always accomplish much, much more than you think before taking that first step. How much you actually achieve and what you can proudly look back on someday – that is first and foremost up to the person you meet every morning in your bathroom mirror: yourself. You are solely responsible for yourself and your actions. Whether in the company, in your family, in sports, or volunteering. If you do epic stuff in a company, it's because you can and because you want it. Yes, it's often exhausting to achieve big goals. But be aware of the fact that being able to do meaningful things is first and foremost a gift. It's a gift you're giving yourself. Because you assume responsibility.

> How much you actually achieve and what you can proudly look back on someday – that is first and foremost up to the person you meet every morning in the mirror of your bathroom: yourself.

How many people are going through life whining all the time? How many people say: I have to go to work, I have to make money, and I can't do what I really want to do, and I'm not growing anymore? I don't know who these people are waiting for. Who is supposed to do it for them? No one else will. Whether in top management or in production, in entertainment or in sports: Once we've realized that we are solely responsible for our own lives, the rest is only a matter of willpower. There is no fate we can just surrender to. Stephen Hawking once said that it's strange that even people who believe everything is predestined by fate look to their left and to their right before crossing the street.

Do Epic Stuff – to me, that's not just a saying the publisher printed on the cover of this book to make it sell. Instead, it is what I hope with all my heart you will do after reading this book. You and every other reader. I'm glad you took the time to actually read this book from cover to cover. You didn't do it for me but for yourself. Now is the time to go out and do your own epic stuff, however you define it for yourself. You will automatically become part of something greater. You will become part of a community of people who probably don't know each other personally but who all have one thing in common: They aren't wasting their lives on this planet but instead they do meaningful things and achieve great goals. So go out and do what you've always wanted to do.

Do it like marketing director Alex and bright star Florian. Perhaps Florian is a better zookeeper than he is a marketer. Or he might not be, and he's just going in a circle to make a new experience and get to know himself better. If so, that's okay, too. Alex knows that. He knows he can't hold Florian back, and he doesn't want too, either. He still vividly remembers the times when a leader would have pulled all the stops in a situation like that: You can't just leave (giving him the guilt trip), we'll pay you more (luring him with bank notes) and you'll soon be given more responsibility (using the power incentive) … Alex doesn't want to do any of that. Of course he doesn't want to lose a great talent. But he knows that if Florian can't see the purpose, if he's not thrilled about what he's doing every day, if the team's goals in this company aren't his cup of tea, then you just can't do epic stuff with him. Then Florian will simply not be happy there. And the last thing Alex wants is to endure the misery of spending his days with unhappy people. Alex wants to see his team members' eyes light up. Yes, in the end, the numbers should also work out. But that's no longer what really matters to him. Being a leader, he wants to initiate something that has to do with the human dreams. And he knows: It's possible!

Just as Carey, who is responsible for IT in a global group, knows it. Carey has disentangled herself from her old, limiting belief systems. When everyone says, "Impossible! That will never work!", she just smiles and stays relaxed. She has understood that the limits of our own imagination restrict us a lot more than any external obstacles do. Carey believes in herself and her own abilities. Unshakeably. It wasn't always like that. In her parents' home and in school, she learned what many are learning there: Life is a struggle, you are hardly ever good enough, and as a woman you must work twice as hard as any man. Today, Carey knows that it's not about struggling. It's not necessary to struggle. For nothing is as strong as the power of a positive vision. Nothing gives you more powerful wings than the belief in yourself, in the attainability of a goal, and in what's possible if you join forces with others. We program our minds for success or failure. It's not a struggle; it's only a decision. Everyone can decide to be successful. And we all have to believe in ourselves.

Like project leader Alain does while standing on a rooftop terrace in the morning and envisioning the future in 4D for his team. For Alain, projects are not the sum of schedules, resources, milestones or FTEs. All that is part of it, no question. Yet Alain knows that it is not these external things people go the extra mile and surpass themselves for. Instead, a better, more pleasant and happier future is what people keep wanting. No man can save the world every day, and we won't create paradise on Earth in six months, either. But if we know there is a worthwhile goal, there is a future state that will make life more beautiful, more pleasant, more joyful or easier for us, our customers and many other people, a state that will give people room to breathe, that will surprise them – if we know that, it will motivate us more than anything to be involved in creating this state. We all dream of a better, more pleasant and happier future. To ensure it doesn't stay a dream, we keep focusing our energy on big goals. That's why we are not happy with half-assed stuff. That's why we want epic stuff.

So do whatever epic stuff means to you. But do it. Now.

Thank You

This book was created with the cooperation of many experts, customers, partners, colleagues – and friends.

I particularly want to thank my family, who showed a lot of patience and understanding. Thank you, Meli, Emmi, and Alicia.

A big thank you to all of you: Carolin Adler, Ludwig Askemper, Kai Czeschlik, Walter Gunz, Jörg Hellwig, Christoph Hüls, Joachim Jäckle, David Jeans, Rahmyn Kress, Susann Kunz, Axel Löber, Dirk Ramhorst, Frank Sielaff, Nils Stamm, Kathie Starks, Martin Stork, Klaus Straub, Daniel Szabo, Lu Yuan.

Thank you so much, Stephanie Walter from Campus Verlag. You're doing an awesome job and it's great fun to create books with you. (Yes, books – there will be more.)

Thank you, Jörg Achim Zoll, Dorothee Köhler, Anthea Stoll, Sonja Weber, David Braga, Jennifer Voss, and Chantal Deussner. Without you, this book would not be what it has become.

Many thanks to Brian Tracy – I learned a lot from you, and I'm even happier that you, as a *New York Times* bestselling author, have provided a testimonial for my book. Thank you very much for that, too!

About the Author

René Esteban is founder and managing director of the consulting firm FocusFirst GmbH. He helps executives and their teams to achieve their most challenging goals in a global corporate environment.

DAX 30 companies will typically bring René and his team into the company when faced with challenges that, due to their size and complexity, initially seem difficult to manage. René and his team will then ensure that there is focus and inspiration. His work is based on expert methods from the field of success psychology, with which large goals can be achieved both faster and more gently.

The question of what makes people successful already fascinated René when he was still a teenager. After completing a commercial apprenticeship, he started to work for a DAX 30 corporation, where he was in charge of global e-commerce in more than 45 countries by the young age of 26. He always kept an eye on the matter that's close to his heart: "goals and success" – and he increasingly used his expert knowledge on that topic in his international teams within the corporation.

In 2016, René founded FocusFirst GmbH. The company is named after what is most important for accomplishing any goal: focus. Within just a few years, several DAX 30 companies were among his clients.

René lives near Frankfurt with his wife, Melanie, and his two daughters, Emilia and Alicia. He loves travelling, getting to know the world, the people he meets and their different cultures.

Interviewees

David Jeans
Owner, Beganya Business
Services & Partner FocusFirst,
former SVP, Merck Life Science

Kathie Starks
Branch Manager
and Head of Asset Servicing,
Bank of New York Mellon

Frank Sielaff
Founder & Managing
Director entrusted,
former Director Digital Media,
Merck Group

Kai Czeschlik
CDO, Allianz
Versicherungs AG

Lu Yuan
Shaolin Master,
head of the Schorndorf
Shaolin Center

Walter Gunz
Co-Founder,
MediaMarkt

Susann Kunz
Director Global Brands Head Office –
Brand Strategy / Business Development,
adidas and Founder,
CEO Academy of Leadership Development

Martin Stork
Head of Workforce
Enablement,
BASF SE

Klaus Straub
Former CIO & Senior Vice President
Information Management,
BMW Group

Dr. Christoph Hüls
Internal Entrepreneur
in Action,
Merck Group

Nils Stamm
CDO, Deutsche Telekom and
former Deputy Chairman,
Münchner Kreis

Daniel Szabo
CEO, Körber Digital and
Founder, YOU MAWO

Dr. Joachim Jäckle
Former CIO & Global Head of
Integrated Business Solutions,
Henkel

Axel Löber
Senior Vice President
Global Brand & Marketing,
E.ON

Jörg Hellwig
CDO,
LANXESS

Ludwig Askemper
Managing Director,
Mondelez Austria

Dr. Rahmyn Kress
HenkelX Ventures and
Founder HenkelX

Index